Jesus: The Antidote to the World's Poison
An inductive study of the book of Colossians

Henry Jackson III
& Christina Joy Hommes

Copyright © 2018 by Henry Jackson III

All rights reserved. No part of this publication may be reproduced, distributed, or transmitted in any form or by any means, including photocopying, recording, or other electronic or mechanical methods, without the prior written permission of the publisher, except in the case of brief quotations embodied in critical reviews and certain other noncommercial uses permitted by copyright law. Submit all permission requests to the publisher via email at publishing@ibible.study.

Ordering Information:
Quantity sales. Special discounts are available on quantity purchases by non-profits, ministries, churches, corporations, associations, and others. For details, contact the publisher via email at sales@ibible.study.

Printed in the United States of America
First Printing, 2018

ISBN 978-1-9835-4348-7

Visit us online at http://ibible.study

Because of the dynamic nature of the internet, any web addresses or links contained in this book may have changed since publication and may no longer be valid.

INDUCTIVE BIBLE STUDY APP

The Inductive Bible Study App inspires people to spend time with God everyday. It is a beautiful, easy to use, full-featured online Bible app with detailed lessons, amazing videos, stories, commentaries, and multiple translations designed for quick navigation, easy note taking, in-depth learning, and powerful Bible study.

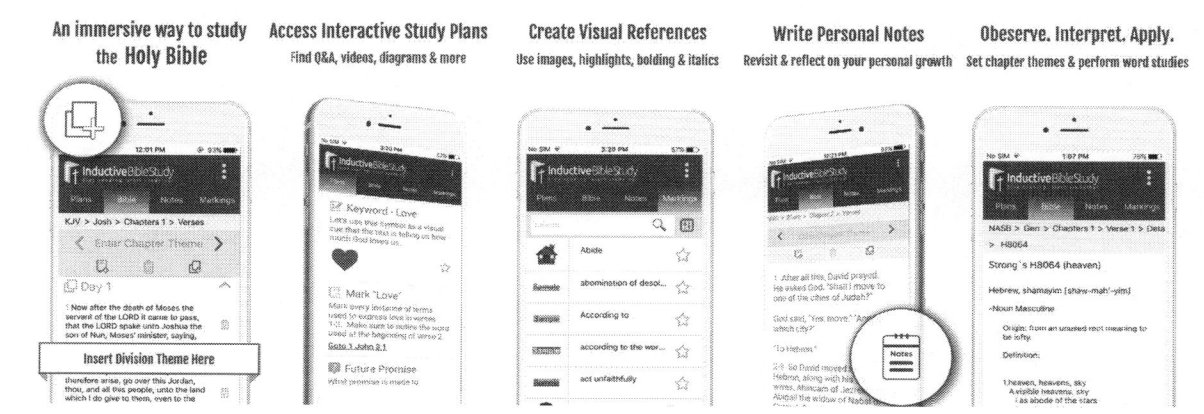

An immersive way to study the Holy Bible

Access Interactive Study Plans
Find Q&A, videos, diagrams & more

Create Visual References
Use images, highlights, bolding & italics

Write Personal Notes
Revisit & reflect on your personal growth

Observe. Interpret. Apply.
Set chapter themes & perform word studies

Download the #1 Free Inductive Bible Study App today!
http://ibstudyapp.com

Available on the App Store | GET IT ON Google Play | Available at amazon apps

Connect with us:

- /InductiveBibleStudyApp
- @iBibleStudyApp
- InductiveBibleStudyApp
- InductiveBibleStudyApp

CONTENTS

Complete	Title	Page
☐	Introduction	6
☐	How to Use This Study Guide	11
☐	About Inductive Bible Study	15
☐	Lesson 1: Hope Changes Everything *Colossians 1:1-8*	21
☐	Lesson 2: A Glimpse into an Effective Prayer Life *Colossians 1:9-12*	41
☐	Lesson 3: The One with First Place *Colossians 1:13-18*	58
☐	Lesson 4: Reconciled by the Cross of Christ *Colossians 1:19-23*	79
☐	Lesson 5: The Mystery of the Gospel *Colossians 1:24-29*	97
☐	Lesson 6: The Minister's Role *Colossians 2:1-5*	116
☐	Lesson 7: Who Jesus Christ Is to a Believer *Colossians 2:6-10*	137
☐	Lesson 8: The 4 Ways Christians Have Victory over Sin *Colossians 2:11-15*	156
☐	Lesson 9: The True Freedom of a Christian *Colossians 2:16-23*	171

Complete	Title	Page
☐	Lesson 10: What Does It Look Like to Be Risen with Christ? *Colossians 3:1-4*	187
☐	Lesson 11: How a Christian Treats Sin *Colossians 3:5-8*	202
☐	Lesson 12: Which Coat Will You Wear Today? *Colossians 3:9-12*	219
☐	Lesson 13: Love – The Key to Every Christian Virtue *Colossians 3:12-17*	232
☐	Lesson 14: The Christian Family *Colossians 3:18-21*	250
☐	Lesson 15: God's Blueprint for Christians in the Workplace *Colossians 3:22-4:1*	266
☐	Lesson 16: 4 Directions for a Healthy Christian Life *Colossians 4:2-6*	284
☐	Lesson 17: Paul's Helpers *Colossians 4:7-11*	300
☐	Lesson 18: Examples of Faithful Servants *Colossians 4:12-18*	317

INTRODUCTION

OBJECTIVE

God's Word is powerful. Through it, He changes the way we think and live. Here are four things we can gain from studying Colossians:
1. Know the Lord Jesus Christ better and be drawn to love Him more
2. Recognize and reject false piety and false religion
3. Understand the victory and new life each Christian has through Christ's death and resurrection and what that looks like in everyday life
4. Broadly understand and recall the structure and content of Colossians and apply its truth to daily life

BOOK IN A SENTENCE

Jesus Christ destroyed the poison and power of sin through His death and offers hope and life through His resurrection.

SUMMARY

In the first half of the book of Colossians, we see Jesus Christ exalted as God, man, and Savior. We also see how Christ's death defeated sin together with the devil, death, and false religion.

In the second half of Colossians, we see how Christ's resurrection impacts His people. It leads them to reject worldly living and instead live lives of holiness, humility, forgiveness, peace, and wisdom with family, in the workplace, in the church, and in public.

THEMES

There are several themes in the book of Colossians. Three that you'll see throughout the book are:
1. The impact and sufficiency of Christ's death and resurrection
2. Sin's defeat through Christ's death and in a believer's life
3. The new life believers have through Christ's resurrection

SUGGESTED MEMORIZATION/MEDITATION PASSAGES

Colossians 1:13-14
Colossians 3:1-4

HIGH LEVEL OUTLINE

1-2 Who Jesus Is and What He Has Done
    1:1-2 Introduction and Greeting
    1:3-12 Paul's Prayer
    1:13-20 Jesus Christ's Identity and Work
    1:21-2:3 The Mystery of the Gospel
    2:4-23 Warning against False Religion

3-4 Who Christ's People Are in Him and What They Should Do
    3:1-4 Christians' Identity
    3:5-9 The Old Nature
    3:10-4:6 The New Nature
    4:7-14 Paul's Helpers
    4:15-18 Closing and Benediction

AUTHOR

In the first verse of Colossians, we're told that the human authors are Paul the apostle and Timothy. Paul had once been a violent persecutor of Christians. After God saved him, Paul became a travelling preacher who told people about the good news of salvation through Jesus the Messiah. Everywhere he went, Paul started churches where believers gathered to worship the Lord. Colossians is one of many letters Paul wrote to various churches which are books of the Bible.

Timothy was a young man who travelled with Paul and became his most trusted helper. Paul often sent Timothy to encourage and teach churches he couldn't visit himself.

Paul penned few of his letters himself. Perhaps because he often wrote them while in prison with his arms chained to Roman soldiers, he usually had scribes. It seems Timothy penned this letter for Paul.

Even more important than Paul or Timothy as authors of Colossians is God. God tells us that He inspired (breathed out) all of Scripture. This means that Colossians, as part of the BIble, is God's Word to us. Since God is the ultimate authority and cannot lie, we know that everything in Colossians is true and must be believed and obeyed.

AUDIENCE AND BACKGROUND

Colossae was located in the region that is modern-day Turkey. It was nearly 100 miles from Ephesus where Paul had spent two years of fruitful ministry. Visitors from Colossae likely heard the gospel in Ephesus and then went back to Colossae to start a church in that city. Paul had never visited the city, but faithfully prayed for the believers there.

Paul received a report in prison (likely during his first imprisonment in Rome) about the spiritual vitality of the Colossian church. He also heard about the false teachers who were trying to convince the Christians in Colossae that they had to add certain practices – like worshipping angels, punishing the body, and observing rituals – to their faith in Jesus Christ for salvation.

Paul wrote this letter to encourage them in their faith, warn them against the false teachers, and remind them who Jesus Christ is.

The Christians in Colossae were the first recipients of this letter, but Paul told them to share it with other churches. God preserved it through the centuries so that you could read and study it now.

In other words, you are the audience of the book of Colossians just as much as those early Colossian believers. Whatever your background and situation, this book is God's message for you today.

How to Use This
STUDY GUIDE

MARKINGS

Each of these studies through the book of Colossians recommends that you mark a keyword or set of keywords that is at the heart of the passage. Marking is a key component of inductive Bible study because it requires you to think about the ideas at the center of each section of the book.

There is a simple marking suggested for each word or words. If you are creative and want to come up with your own marking to help you better remember or think about the key concept, go for it!

You can find a printable Bible worksheet containing the text of each passage on our website (http://ibible.study/worksheet). By downloading this worksheet, you can mark as much as you like even if you don't want to have the markings in your Bible forever.

PACE

One beautiful thing about this inductive Bible study of Colossians is that you can work at your own pace. This is not a timed study curriculum. You can do a study in one sitting or several. You can study a new passage every day or once a week – whatever works best for you. The most important thing is not how often you finish these studies or how long they take, but whether you are committed to regularly listening to God in His Word and doing what He says.

SMALL GROUP OR INDEPENDENT STUDY

Whether you want to study the Bible alone or with others, this book is designed to help you. Each study will help you explore a short portion of Colossians as you consider what it says and what that means for your life.

Because each study takes you on a journey through the passage, you do not need training or experience as a leader or Bible teacher to use this with a friend or study group. You can all work through the study together, discussing the answers to the questions. Or, each member of the group can work individually through the passage using the study guide and then share insights and ideas when you gather.

Another resource you may find helpful is the Inductive Bible Study App. In the app, you'll find similar study plans for each passage. By using the app with this book you can do the markings in the app and quickly access referenced passages.

STYLE

With a combination of devotional and in-depth Bible study, these studies will deepen your grasp of each passage while helping you see how God is calling you to change your life to be more like Christ. The variety of question types will help you explore Colossians and remember what you find. This book is designed to be compact so you can study the Bible in your favorite place.

These studies can only provide a starting point as you explore God's Word. Only a few themes from each passage can feature in this book. When other topics stand out to you, you can add your own thoughts and applications in the margins.

ONE MORE THOUGHT

Colossians will challenge you many times regarding your faith. Do you fully accept everything God says about Himself and you? Have you trusted in Jesus' death on your behalf to pay the debt of your sins so that you do not have to die for them? Does your life demonstrate this faith in Christ through obedience and love?

Your salvation is the most important thing since it determines your relationship with God and your eternal destiny. Everything else hardly matters if you do not have eternal life through Jesus Christ. So take time to wrestle with these questions as you study Colossians.

We pray that if you don't know the joy of loving and worshiping the Lord Jesus, you will by the end of this study. If you already know Him, we pray that your joy will be deepened as you grow to know Him more and find greater assurance of your faith.

SHARE YOUR THOUGHTS

Send us feedback (feedback@ibible.study) to let us know how these studies have been a blessing to you in your walk with God.

About Inductive BIBLE STUDY

Inductive Bible study asks the Bible to speak for itself. Instead of coming to the Bible to prove certain points or demonstrate conclusions we've already reached, inductive study allows God's Word to direct our thinking and control our beliefs.

To do this, we come to the Bible with humility and faith, asking questions to understand its meaning. This search opens with prayer, is divided into three parts – observation, interpretation, and application – and continues through meditation and memory.

PRAYER

Scripture teaches us that we cannot fully understand it on our own without the Holy Spirit teaching us what it means. Because of this, we come to God in prayer before we read and study the Bible. When we pray before seeking Him in His Word, we humble ourselves before God. We ask Him to help us lay aside our wrong ideas, to expose our sinful thoughts and actions, to show us what He wants us to believe and how He wants us to live, and to show us the wonderful truths and promises He has placed in His Word for us.

OBSERVATION

The next step after we have asked God to open our eyes and teach us through His Word is to read the passage and observe what it says. Have you ever watched a little child observe a new scene? Perhaps he is at a petting zoo and tells you all about it: "There is a lamb. She's so cute. Do you see how that little girl is petting her? And look at that rooster. Isn't his red crown funny! Does he crow like the roosters in my books? Oh! Do you see the little chicks…" He is observing his surroundings.

This is exactly what we should do when we read a passage of Scripture. We notice:

- Who is mentioned?
- When or where did events occur?
- What happened or is taught?
- Why did it happen, or why does God give us that command?
- How does it compare with other verses around it?
- What is the central message or theme of the passage?
- And other similar questions.

As we ask these questions, we become familiar with what the passage says.

INTERPRETATION

Once we have observed what the passage says, we next ask questions to understand what it means.

- We explore the concepts and commands in the passage to better understand them.
- We ask why each element is significant.
- We study words that stand out to us or that we don't understand.
- We search other parts of God's Word to gain a broader understanding of the ideas and commands in the passage.

Sometimes we turn to other resources to help us assemble and summarize the Bible's teachings on a topic. It is important to remember that these tools are not perfect. We should be careful to choose resources created to teach what the Bible says without adding to it or taking away from it.

One of the most important things to remember as we interpret the Bible is that all of it points to Jesus Christ. The Bible is God's revelation of Himself to us. We see all of these truths about God and how they should impact our earthly lives displayed perfectly in the life of His

Son Jesus Christ. He is the reason we can be forgiven and made right with God, the center of the gospel, and the ultimate example of everything the Bible teaches. As we look for how everything points us to Him, we will begin to understand God's Word better.

APPLICATION

Now that we understand the passage, it is critical to obey it. God warns us not to hear His Word without taking action. Every time we read and think about Scripture we should ask, "What does God want me to do about this?"

This application of the Bible's truths must be personal and practical. It isn't enough to know what people generally should do about it, we must ask how God wants to change our lives and relationships today. When we have discovered what needs to change, we should plan very specific action steps so we can begin to obey God's Word and receive His blessings.

A STEP FURTHER

Once we've inductively studied a passage, it can be easy to feel we understand and know it. In reality, we've only scratched the surface. God's Word is like a treasure mine that never runs out of gems. Every time we dig, we find more.

That is why we read and study the Bible over and over again. It is also the reason God has commanded us to meditate on and memorize His Word. Christian meditation is concentrating on a verse or phrase from the Bible for a while – keeping it in your mind and thinking about it. Purposefully thinking God's thoughts by thinking His Word changes our minds and lives to make us like the Lord Jesus.

One of the easiest ways to meditate on a passage is to memorize it. By doing this we obey two of God's commands – to meditate on His Word and to memorize it. Memorizing Bible verses can be as simple as writing a verse out and reading it through the day, repeating phrases of it to yourself and thinking about them. After a while, the phrases will stick in your mind.

As you study Colossians, certain verses may stand out to you. These would be good verses to meditate on and memorize.

Lessons

Hope Changes EVERYTHING

LESSON 1

BIG IDEA

The hope of the future that God has prepared for every believer changes everything about the way they live.

PASSAGE

Colossians 1:1-8

TOPIC

Hope

INTRODUCTION

In 1981, the successful millionaire Eugene Land was asked to address a class of 59 sixth graders in East Harlem, NY. He asked the school's principal how many of the students would likely go to college. After hearing that perhaps one student might, Eugene felt their despair.

Finally the moment came, and Eugene stood before the students wondering if he could even hold eye contact. With sudden inspiration he set aside his notes and told each student:

"Stay in school, and I'll pay the college tuition for every one of you."

An amazing 90 percent of that class graduated from high school. Why? Because they had hope. One of the students commented, "I had something to look forward to, something waiting for me. It was a golden feeling."

In Colossians 1:1-8, we are told about a hope which awaits every believer and changes their life. Study the passage to learn more about this wonderful expectation and how it changes everything.

OBSERVATION

1 › PRAY

Since this is the Word of the living God, ask Him to open your eyes to the truth of this passage. Ask Him to show you how it should impact your life. Tell Him that you desire to be changed.

2 › READ FOCUS VERSES

Read Colossians 1:1–8, and try to understand the main point of these opening verses.

3 › KEYWORD – HOPE

Mark the intangible nouns (words like *faith*, *hope*, *love*, *grace*, and others) in these first 8 verses of the book of Colossians with a plus sign ("**+**") to highlight their prominent role in the passage.

Visit **http://ibible.study/worksheet**
to print out a Bible Worksheet for this study.

4 AUTHORS

The human author of this Epistle were _____ and Timothy (also known by his Greek name, Timotheus).

5 RECIPIENTS

Who were the first recipients of this Letter?
- ○ The Jews scattered through the Roman Empire
- ○ The church still in Jerusalem
- ○ The Christians in Colossae
- ○ We aren't told

6 APOSTLESHIP

Why was Paul an apostle according to verse 1?

7 TWO RESPONSES

What two things does Paul say he does continually for these Colossian believers in verse 3?

Gives _____ and _____

Hope Changes Everything | Colossians 1:1-8

8 GOOD BEGINNINGS

When does verse 4 explain that Paul began giving thanks and praying for the Colossian believers?

9 REASONS

What is the reason Paul gives in verse 5 that he can give thanks for them and pray for them?

- ○ Because of the hope stored up for them
- ○ Because of their love for him
- ○ Because of their circumstances

Hope Changes Everything | Colossians 1:1-8

10 GOSPEL RESULTS

What result did the gospel have in the lives of these believers, according to verse 6?

11 MINISTER

Which minister brought the truth of the gospel to the Colossians?

- ○ Timothy
- ○ Epaphras
- ○ Paul
- ○ Epaphroditus

Hope Changes Everything | Colossians 1:1-8

12 EPAPHRAS

How does Paul describe Epaphras?

13 REPORT

What report of these Christians did Epaphras bring to Paul, according to verse 8?

14 | WHO'S WHO?

Based on the passage, match the people with their activities:

Church in Colossae ○   ○ Apostle of Jesus Christ
Epaphras ○   ○ Referred to as "our brother"
Timothy ○   ○ Faithful brothers and sisters
Paul ●----------● Faithful minister of Christ

15 | WHICH ORDER?

See if you can place the events represented in this passage in sequence.

- ☐ Colossians understand the grace of God
- ☐ Paul & Timothy write a letter to the Colossians
- ☑ [1] Epaphras preached the gospel in Colossae
- ☐ Paul and Timothy hear of the faith of the Colossians from Epaphras
- ☐ Epaphras observes the love of the Colossians

INTERPRETATION

1 — PAUL AN APOSTLE

Paul's story is dramatic. When we first meet him in the book of Acts, he was called Saul, and was persecuting, imprisoning, and killing Christians. As he went to capture more Christians in the city of Damascus, God stopped him and changed his life. A light appeared to him from heaven on that road to Damascus. Jesus confronted him for his persecution of Christians and sent him into the city – blind.

After being healed of his blindness, Paul, as he was now known, was commissioned to take the gospel to the Gentile (non-Jewish) world. He travelled thousands of miles to tell people about salvation through Jesus Christ despite being beaten, imprisoned, stoned, and hated. He wrote thirteen books of the Bible by direction of the Holy Spirit. Colossians is one of those books written as a letter to the church in Colossae.

2 EPAPHRAS

Paul mentions Epaphras again at the end of the book. Read what he says about him in Colossians 4:12.

3 STRIKING CHARACTERISTIC

What was so evident about Epaphras' attitude that Paul mentions it as a defining characteristic in both the beginning and end of the book?

- ○ He was gracious
- ○ He was eloquent
- ○ He was kind
- ○ He was a servant

4 | FAITH, HOPE, LOVE

In verses 4-5, Paul speaks of the faith, hope, and love of these believers. Notice how the three are compared in 1 Corinthians 13:13.

5 | FAITH AND LOVE

Read 2 Thessalonians 1:3 and compare it with Colossians 1:4.

6 | FULLER UNDERSTANDING

What characteristics of faith and love do these passages highlight?

Hope Changes Everything | Colossians 1:1-8

7 | HOPE

Verses 5-6 in today's passage speak of a hope which produces fruit in a believer's life. Notice how Titus 2:13-14 expands on this theme.

8 | HOPE'S IMPACT

What impact does the hope of Christ appearing with a reward for believers have on their lives?

9 | LAID UP

Notice the similarities between Colossians 1:5 and 1 Peter 1:3-5.

Hope Changes Everything | Colossians 1:1-8

10 TREASURER

Who is the treasurer of these things laid up for God's people, according to 1 Peter 1:3-5?

11 TRUTH

Verses 5 and 6 both speak of truth. See the theme repeated in Ephesians 1:13-14.

Hope Changes Everything | Colossians 1:1-8

12 LOOK AGAIN

In both of these passages, what is referred to as the truth?

13 CLOSER LOOK

Take a look at the word translated *gospel* (G2098 – euaggelion) in verse 5. It means good news and refers to the glad message of salvation through Jesus Christ.

14 FELLOW SERVANT

Another significant word in this passage is used to describe Epaphras as a *fellow servant* (G4889 – syndoulos). The word refers to another servant who also serves your master, in this case a colleague in Christ's service who obeys His commands.

APPLICATION

1 — A RECORD

If you were living back in the days of Paul, and God had him write about you in the Bible, what kind of record would be written about you? What are you going to do about that today?

2 A TESTIMONY

If you were living back in the days of Paul, and someone brought a record to him about how you were doing as part of your church, what would they have to say, and what are you going to do about that today?

3 SERVANT

Paul considered himself a servant of Jesus Christ, and he calls Epaphras a fellow servant of the same Master. In what ways will truly believing that you are a servant of Jesus Christ and fellow servant to His ministers show in your daily life?

CLOSING

We hope this study has helped you understand the hope of every believer and how it changes everything for them.

JOURNAL

Write down any additional thoughts that come to mind as a result of this lesson.

Additional RESOURCES

To aid in your study of this passage, we've placed the following additional resources on our website:

Paul an Apostle – Watch this short video to get a little background about the apostle Paul.

Colossae – See where Colossae is in modern-day Turkey.

Colossians – Listening through the book of Colossians will help you notice its broader themes and see the wonderful truths it deals with. You might consider listening through it every day during this study to familiarize yourself with its glorious message. You can even listen while you do other simple tasks.

Visit http://ibible.study/resources

A Glimpse into an Effective PRAYER LIFE

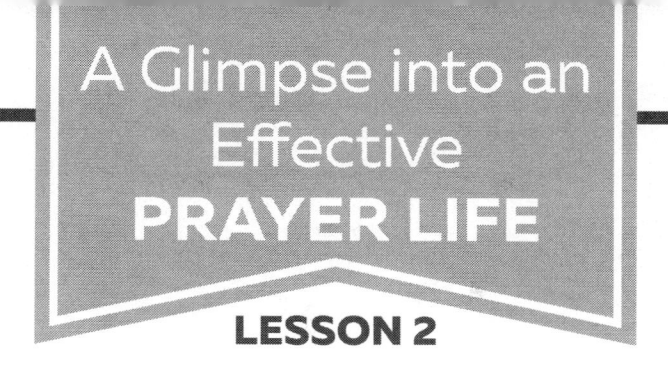

LESSON 2

BIG IDEA

Get a glimpse into Paul's prayer life to jumpstart your own.

PASSAGE

Colossians 1:9–12

TOPIC

Prayer

INTRODUCTION

George Mueller is well known for his effective prayer life. He supported thousands of orphans without ever asking anyone for supplies or even making the needs known. Instead, he daily asked his heavenly Father to supply the things his family and ministry needed.

Even George Mueller struggled to pray at times. He would rise and begin praying as soon as possible, but his mind would often wander for 15-30 minutes before he could focus on prayer.

Eventually, he began to read the Bible before praying. In that habit he found the key to unlocking effective prayer. It prepared his heart, and gave his prayers substance.

Do you struggle to pray? Colossians 1:9-12 gives us a glimpse of the prayer life of the apostle Paul. It will challenge how you pray, and jumpstart your prayer life if you use it as a guide. Are you ready to learn to pray?

OBSERVATION

1 PRAY

Before reading and seeking to understand this passage, ask God to illumine your mind and give you understanding and wisdom through it.

2 READ FOCUS VERSES

Read Colossians 1:9-12 and notice what ties the passage together.

3 ONE THING

What is happening in these verses (hint: look at verse 9)?

A Glimpse into an Effective Prayer Life | Colossians 1:9-12

4 | KEYWORD – PRAY

Mark the word *pray* in verse 9 with a star ("★") so that you will remember this passage is Paul's prayer for these believers.

Visit **http://ibible.study/worksheet** to print out a Bible Worksheet for this study.

5 | GET SOME CONTEXT

Read the verses around today's passage – Colossians 1:3-23 – for context and to gain perspective on this prayer.

6 | WHO?

Who is praying for whom?

- ○ Paul and Barnabas for the church at Jerusalem
- ○ The church at Jerusalem for Paul and Silas
- ○ Paul and Timothy for the church at Colossae
- ○ The church at Colossae for Paul and Titus

7 WHOM?

Are the people Paul is praying for believers in Jesus Christ or unbelievers? How do you know from the passage?

8 WHEN?

Paul began to pray for these Christians as soon as he heard about their faith.

○ True
○ False

A Glimpse into an Effective Prayer Life | Colossians 1:9-12

9 | DESIRE

In what order does Paul mention his desires for these believers in his prayers for them?

- ☐ Increase in the knowledge of God
- ☐ Be fruitful in every good work
- ☐ Be filled with the knowledge of God's will with wisdom and spiritual understanding
- ☐ Be strengthened by God's glorious power for patience, endurance, and joyfulness
- ☐ Walk worthy of the Lord to please Him
- ☐ Give thanks to God the Father

10 | KNOWLEDGE

Which two kinds of knowledge does God especially highlight as important for the believer through Paul's inspired prayer?

- ○ Knowledge of God's will
- ○ Knowledge of heaven
- ○ Knowledge of other Christians
- ○ Knowledge of God

A Glimpse into an Effective Prayer Life | Colossians 1:9-12

11 EQUIPPED

Match each gift Paul requests for these believers with the way it will be evidenced in their lives:

Knowledge of God's will ○   ○ Patience, endurance, joyfulness, and giving thanks

Walk worthy of the Lord ○   ○ Fruitful in good works and increasing knowledge of God

Strengthened with God's power ○   ○ Wisdom and spiritual understanding

12 GOD

Which of God the Father's works are emphasized in verse 12?

A Glimpse into an Effective Prayer Life | Colossians 1:9–12

INTERPRETATION

1 ANOTHER PRAYER

Paul prays a similar prayer for the Ephesian believers in Ephesians 1:15-23. Notice that he started praying for them as soon as he heard about their faith, too.

2 WISDOM AND UNDERSTANDING

In verse 9, we see that the knowledge of God's will comes from wisdom and spiritual understanding. See what Proverbs 9:10 says about the beginning of wisdom and understanding.

3 BEGINNING

What is the beginning of wisdom?

4 TRANSFORMED

Romans 12:2 explains how we come to know and live God's will.

5 RENEWED

How does a person come to know God's will?
- ○ Studying to know themselves better
- ○ Renewing their mind with Scripture
- ○ Listening to the world's wisdom
- ○ Doing what feels right

6 WALKING WORTHY

In Ephesians 4:1-3, we see a little bit more detail about how we are to walk worthy of the Lord.

7 HOW?

How is a believer to walk worthy of the Lord and the calling He has given?

8 PLEASING THE LORD

Verse 10 says that those who walk worthy of the Lord please Him. One example of a man who pleased God is found in Hebrews 11:5.

9 · PLEASING GOD

Stop and consider what a wonder it is that a believer can please God! Considering who God is, why is this so amazing?

10 · FRUITFUL

See what Philippians 1:9-11 says about a fruitful Christian.

11 · TO WHAT END?

Supply the missing word(s) in this summary of Philippians 1:11:

A fruitful Christian brings _____ to God.

A Glimpse into an Effective Prayer Life | Colossians 1:9-12

12 GOOD WORKS

Colossians 1:10 speaks of being fruitful in every good work. See how Ephesians 2:8-10 develops the theme of good works.

13 NOT WORKS

According to Ephesians 2:8, what can works not do?

14 PLEASING THE LORD

Good works cannot save a person, but once they have been saved, how will they live, according to Ephesians 2:10? Why?

15 ETERNAL LIFE

Colossians 1:10 talks about knowing God. Note what John 17:3 says about knowing God.

16 KNOWING GOD

What is the result of truly knowing God?

17 STRENGTHENED

Paul prays in verse 11 that the believers will be strengthened. Romans 8:11 explains who strengthens a believer.

A Glimpse into an Effective Prayer Life | Colossians 1:9–12

18 — WHO?

Who strengthens a believer?

[   ]

19 — WHAT DID HE DO?

What did the Holy Spirit do that demonstrates the greatness of His strength which works through believers?

- ○ Worked miracles through the apostles
- ○ Descended at Jesus' baptism
- ○ Raised Jesus from the dead
- ○ Came at Pentecost

20 — GIVING THANKS

Verse 12 speaks of giving thanks. A couple of chapters later, in Colossians 3:17, we are told when to give thanks.

21 — WHEN?

When are we to give thanks?

22 — INHERITANCE

God has made Christians partakers of an inheritance, according to verse 12. Read in Romans 8:16-17 about whose inheritance it is that Christians will share.

23 — SHARING

Whose inheritance does a Christian share?
- ○ Abraham's
- ○ Jesus'
- ○ Noah's
- ○ Paul's

A Glimpse into an Effective Prayer Life | Colossians 1:9-12

APPLICATION

1 PRAYER

How will what you have studied in this passage impact how you pray for other believers?

2 INHERITANCE

If you lived today like you were about to inherit everything with Jesus, what would your day look like?

CLOSING

We hope this study has given you a glimpse into Paul's prayer life, and jump-started your own.

JOURNAL

Write down any additional thoughts that come to mind as a result of this lesson.

The One with FIRST PLACE

LESSON 3

BIG IDEA

Because God has made His Son, Jesus Christ, preeminent in everything, He must have first place in our lives.

PASSAGE

Colossians 1:13-18

TOPIC

Jesus Christ

INTRODUCTION

If you were to paint a picture of someone famous in a group of other people, would you paint the main subject first or last?

When the German artist, Adolf von Menzel, was painting a portrayal of Frederick the Great speaking with his generals before a famous battle, he decided to paint Fredrick last. Menzel carefully crafted the background and grandly depicted the various generals to create the perfect setting into which to place Frederick.

However, Menzel ran out of time. He died before the painting was finished. Because of his method of leaving the most important element for last, the central subject of Menzel's painting was only outlined in charcoal.

Ironically, the chief subject of the painting was left until it was too late.

Perhaps you are doing the same thing in your life without even thinking about it. Colossians 1:13-18 shows that Christ has first place in everything. Have you made Him first in your life, or will you wait until it is too late? Study this glorious passage to learn more about three ways Christ has been exalted, and how He is preeminent over everything.

OBSERVATION

1 | PRAY

Before reading and studying this amazing passage from God's Word, stop and ask Him to open the eyes of your heart to understand and believe the truths He has written.

2 | READ FOCUS VERSES

Read Colossians 1:13-18 and notice how the passage builds to a climax.

3 | KEY CHARACTER

Who is the main character in this passage?
- ○ Paul
- ○ Timothy
- ○ Epaphras
- ○ Jesus Christ

The One with First Place | Colossians 1:13-18

4 CLIMAX

Add the keyword to complete this summary of the climax at the end of verse 18:

In all things Jesus has the _____

5 CONTEXT

Read Colossians 1:9-20 for a slightly broader perspective on today's passage and how it fits in the book of Colossians.

6 KEYWORDS – WHO JESUS IS

Mark with a cross ("†") all the things in Colossians 1:13-18 that God says His Son, Jesus Christ, is or has done.

Visit **http://ibible.study/worksheet**
to print out a Bible Worksheet for this study.

7 HOW MANY?

How many things do these 6 verses say about the person and work of Jesus Christ?

8 DELIVERED AND PLANTED

Match the pairs:

Delivered from ○   ○ Kingdom of Jesus Christ

Planted in ○   ○ Kingdom of darkness

9 THROUGH HIS BLOOD

According to verse 14, what two things do believers have through Jesus Christ's blood?

_____ and _____ of sins

The One with First Place | Colossians 1:13–18

10 IMAGE

Jesus is the image of the invisible God.
- ○ True
- ○ False

11 CREATOR

Put the following list of things Jesus Christ created in their order from verse 16:

- ☐ Dominions
- ☐ Things in heaven
- ☐ Powers
- ☐ Visible things
- ☐ Rulers
- ☐ Things on earth
- ☐ Invisible things
- ☐ All things
- ☐ Thrones

12 PREEXISTENCE

When does verse 17 say that Jesus Christ existed?

- ○ Since his birth
- ○ Before all things
- ○ Since creation
- ○ Unclear

13 HEAD

Why is Christ exalted in everything, according to verse 18?

The One with First Place | Colossians 1:13-18

INTERPRETATION

1 — 3 WAYS

Colossians 1:13-18 speaks of three ways Christ is preeminent because of His works.

Match (1) each of the ways Christ has first place with (2) the part of His work that earned or demonstrates that preeminence and (3) the verse numbers that tell us about each:

Over God's kingdom	Because He is risen from the dead	vv. 15-17
He is God	Because of His work of redemption	v. 18
Head of the church	Shown by His work of creation	vv. 13-14

The One with First Place | Colossians 1:13-18

2 SUMMARY

We've seen that Christ is exalted over God's kingdom, over all creation, and over the church. How does the end of verse 18 summarize the ways Christ is preeminent?

3 POWER OF DARKNESS

Verse 13 speaks of God taking Christians out of the power of darkness and translating them into the kingdom of His dear Son. See how Ephesians 6:11-13 helps us understand the darkness from which God has delivered His people.

4 BELOVED

The Lord Jesus is referred to as God's dear Son in today's passage. Notice how God speaks of Him in John 3:16.

5 LOVE

How does understanding God's perfect love for His Son emphasize to us how much He loves us?

6 FORGIVENESS

Read Ephesians 1:7-8 and notice that it is very similar to Colossians 1:14.

7 CHRIST'S BLOOD

Why are Christians redeemed and forgiven through Christ's blood?

8 INVISIBLE GOD

Throughout the Bible, God is described as invisible because He dwells in light which no one can approach. See what He says about people seeing Him in Exodus 33:20.

9 EXACT IMAGE

All people are made in the image of God, but Jesus Christ is not just an image-bearer. See what Hebrews 1:3 says about him.

10 GOD'S IMAGE

Because Jesus is the image of God, notice what He said to His disciples in John 14:9.

11 WHO IS HE?

If Jesus is the exact image of God such that you have seen God when you have seen Him, who must He be?

12 | FIRSTBORN

How can Jesus be both the image of God, who is Creator of everything, and the firstborn over all creation? The word *firstborn* in the Bible is used both to signify birth order (as in Jesus being the firstborn son of Mary) and rank (as in David – a youngest son and second king – being God's firstborn in Psalm 89:27). Jesus ranks before all creation.

13 | CREATOR

John 1:1-3 is very similar to Colossians 1:15-17.

14 | PARALLELS

What are some of the parallels between these two passages?

15 GOD CREATED

Take a careful look at Genesis 1:1.

16 WHO IS JESUS?

If God created everything and Jesus Christ created everything, who is Jesus Christ?

17 HEAD OF THE CHURCH

Ephesians 1:22-23 also speaks of Christ as the Head of the church.

18 SIGNIFICANCE

What does it mean that Christ is the head of the church, and why is that significant in this passage about Christ's preeminence?

19 FIRST RAISED

Romans 8:11 explains why it is so important for Christ to be the first raised to eternal life.

20 IMPORTANT

Why is it important that Christ is the first raised from the dead to eternal life?

The One with First Place | Colossians 1:13–18

21 | PREEMINENCE

Take a moment to consider the simple clarity of the word translated *preeminent* or *first place* (G4409 – prōteuō). It means to be first or have first place in rank or influence.

22 | SEEKING PREEMINENCE

In 3 John 1:9, we are told about a man who wanted to be preeminent in the church.

23 | PROBLEM

Based on today's passage in Colossians, why was it a problem for Diotrephes to want preeminence in the church?

24 HIGH OVER ALL

The hymn "Jesus the Name High Over All" by Charles Wesley worships Christ as preeminent in His work of redemption.

Jesus, the name high over all,
In hell, or earth, or sky:
Angels and men before it fall,
And devils fear and fly.

Jesus, the name to sinners dear,
The name to sinners giv'n;
It scatters all their guilty fear,
It turns their hell to heav'n.

Jesus the prisoner's fetters breaks,
And bruises Satan's head;
Pow'r into strengthless souls He speaks,
And life into the dead.

Oh, that the world might taste and see,
The riches of His grace!

The arms of love that compass me,
Would all mankind embrace.

His only righteousness I show,
His saving grace proclaim:
'Tis all my business here below,
To cry, "Behold the Lamb!"

Happy, if with my latest breath
I may but gasp His name:
Preach Him to all, and cry in death,
"Behold, behold the Lamb!"

The One with First Place | Colossians 1:13-18

APPLICATION

1 WHO'S FIRST

Who has preeminence in your life?

2 PUTTING JESUS CHRIST FIRST

What will it look like to acknowledge Jesus Christ's rightful position and put Him first in your life today?

CLOSING

We hope this study has challenged you to give Christ first place in your life and worship Him as the Son of God.

JOURNAL

Write down any additional thoughts that come to mind as a result of this lesson.

The One with First Place | Colossians 1:13-18

Additional RESOURCES

To aid in your study of this passage, we've placed the following additional resources on our website:

Firstborn – This short discussion further explains how Jesus is both the image of God and the firstborn over all creation as presented in Colossians 1:15.

Jesus the Name High Over All – Listen to this hymn as you worship the One who has first place.

Visit http://ibible.study/resources

Reconciled by the CROSS OF CHRIST

LESSON 4

BIG IDEA

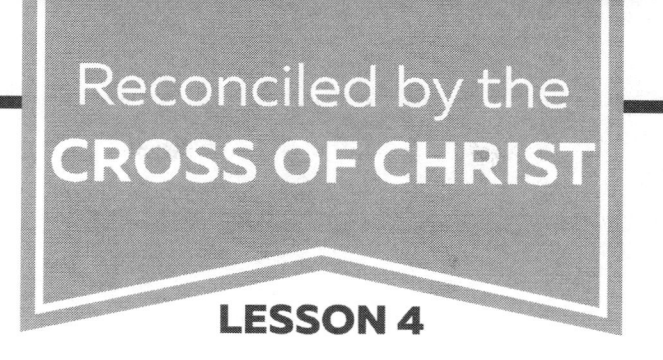

Sinners can be reconciled to God through Christ's death and are called to continue in the faith.

PASSAGE

Colossians 1:19-23

TOPIC

Salvation

INTRODUCTION

Have you ever had to reconcile with someone? Somehow you hurt or wronged them and the relationship was estranged. Then, through repentance and making things right, you were able to restore a relationship. Perhaps someone else mediated the reconciliation between you and your friend.

Two men who have greatly impacted the modern church gave their lives in effort to reconcile people. Martin Luther, the great reformer, died after becoming ill on his way home from mediating reconciliation between two estranged brothers. John Bunyan, author of *Pilgrim's Progress*, died while mediating between an estranged father and son.

In another case, a man and his wife became estranged and each moved to distant portions of the country. The man eventually had business back in his hometown. While there, he went to the cemetery to visit the grave of his only son. A footstep behind him recalled him from fond memories. There stood his wife who had also come to visit the grave. That day they were reconciled because of their common interest in their son who was dead.

These stories are a little picture of the broken relationship between every person and God. Those whose deaths facilitated reconciliation are a small picture of the work of Jesus Christ who died to reconcile sinners to God. Colossians 1:19-23 speaks of Christ's work of reconciliation. Learn more about this beautiful reality as you study these verses.

OBSERVATION

1 — PRAY

As you begin to study this passage of Scripture, go to God and ask Him to make it clear to you. Ask Him to give you wisdom through it and to show you what must change in your life so that you can please Him. He will increase your understanding as you ask for it in humility.

2 — READ FOCUS VERSES

Carefully read Colossians 1:19-23. Pay attention to what it says about Christ's work and how it applies to your life.

3 CONTEXT

Colossians 1 is a very connected passage. The verses are tightly woven together and communicate a unified message. To understand today's passage better, read it in context by reading Colossians 1:13-23.

4 KEYWORD – JESUS

Use a cross ("†") again to mark each word having to do with Jesus in Colossians 1:19-23. Don't forget the pronouns (like *He, Him, His*).

Visit **http://ibible.study/worksheet**
to print out a Bible Worksheet for this study.

5 KEYWORD – RECONCILE

Use an up arrow–down arrow ("↑↓") to mark the word *reconcile* which appears twice in this passage and serves a key role in explaining these verses.

6 FULLNESS

In whom does all the fullness of God dwell, according to verse 19?

7 THE CROSS

What does verse 20 say that the cross brings?

○ Joy
○ Peace
○ Love
○ Faith

8 ESTRANGED

What estranges people from God, according to verse 21?

- ○ Misunderstandings
- ○ Nothing particular
- ○ Mistakes
- ○ Wicked works

9 RECONCILED

How was that estrangement ended for God's people, according to verses 21-22?

Through the _____ of Jesus Christ

10 — THROUGH DEATH

How does verse 22 say Christ presents His people to the Father because of His death?

11 — EVIDENCE

A true Christian will never move away from the gospel, but will persevere in faith (verse 23).

- ○ True
- ○ False

INTERPRETATION

1 | FULLNESS

Colossians 1:19 is further explained by Colossians 2:9. Read the passage and notice the connection.

2 | WHO HE IS

If someone asked you how you know that Jesus is God, how could you use these verses to answer their question?

Reconciled by the Cross of Christ | Colossians 1:19-23

3 ENEMIES

Romans 5:10 also speaks of us as enemies who were reconciled by Christ's death.

4 RECONCILIATION

This passage speaks of Christ reconciling us to God. The word translated *reconcile* (G604 – apokatallassō) is a strong term. It means to restore peace or harmony between estranged parties.

5 FILTHY RAGS

Perhaps you consider yourself a pretty good person. You may not feel that you've done a lot of wicked works (verse 21) which would have estranged you from God. Read Isaiah 64:6 to get God's perspective on your works.

Reconciled by the Cross of Christ | Colossians 1:19-23

6 ANOTHER PIECE

Romans 6:23 will add one more piece of the puzzle to explain why Christ's death was required for this reconciliation.

7 DEATH

When you put all of these passages together, why did Christ have to die so that people could be reconciled to God?

8 — MADE HOLY

Colossians 1:22 and 2 Corinthians 5:21 both show that the reconciliation Christ works between people and God is more than taking away the guilt of sin. What is also necessary for people to be accepted by God?

- ○ The righteousness of Christ
- ○ A positive attitude
- ○ Good works
- ○ Money or fame

9 — RECONCILED TO GOD

2 Corinthians 5:17-21 expands on the idea of our being reconciled to God. Read the passage slowly taking time to think about how God brought about reconciliation between Himself and sinful people who were His enemies.

10 | TAKING ROOT

In His parable of the soils in Luke 8:4-15, Jesus teaches that true Christians continue in the faith.

11 | CONTINUE

In Colossians 1:23, we see that an evidence of a true believer is continuing in the faith and hope of the gospel. This is one of the main themes of the book of Hebrews. Read Hebrews 3:13-14 to see its warning that a true believer must persevere.

12 | LOOK-ALIKES

According to these passages, a person can look like a Christian in the beginning even though they aren't one for real.

○ True
○ False

13 THE DIFFERENCE

From these passages, how would you explain the difference between a true believer and someone who looks like one?

Reconciled by the Cross of Christ | Colossians 1:19-23

APPLICATION

1 RECONCILED TO GOD

Have you been reconciled to God as this passage describes it? Why do you say that?

2 PERSEVERANCE

As you look at your life, do you see your faith increasing and rooting down into Christ, or has your faith been shaken by troubles? What is the next step you will take based on this study?

Reconciled by the Cross of Christ | Colossians 1:19-23

3 · MINISTRY OF RECONCILIATION

If you have been reconciled to God and are holding fast to Christ by faith, 2 Corinthians 5 says that you have a ministry of reconciliation in calling others to be reconciled to God. How will you fulfill that ministry today?

CLOSING

We hope this study has given you a better understanding of Christ's work of reconciliation between people and God and has challenged you to continue in the faith.

JOURNAL

Write down any additional thoughts that come to mind as a result of this lesson.

Additional RESOURCES

To aid in your study of this passage, we've placed the following additional resource on our website:

His Robes for Mine – From these verses we see that in salvation a wonderful exchange is made. Christ takes the sinner's sin and guilt along with its penalty of death. But that is not enough to reconcile a sinner to a holy God. Christ's righteousness is given to the sinner in exchange for his sins so that now it is like he is spotlessly righteous as Christ is. This hymn expands on that glorious truth.

Visit http://ibible.study/resources

The Mystery of **THE GOSPEL**

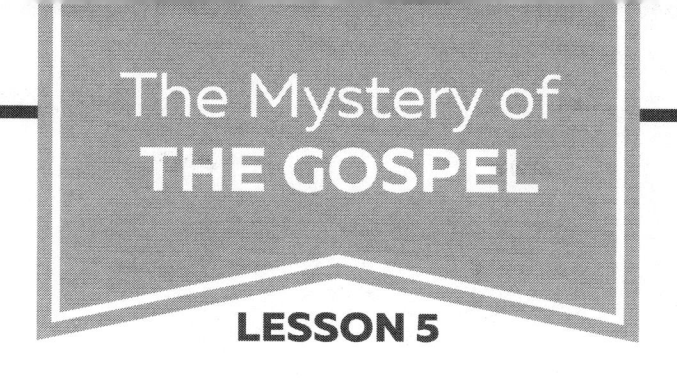

LESSON 5

BIG IDEA

God has revealed the mystery of the gospel which He empowers Christians to share with everyone.

PASSAGE

Colossians 1:24–29

TOPIC

Gospel

INTRODUCTION

Once the famous artist Thomas Nast held a public exhibition. On his canvas, which was about six feet by two feet, appeared a farmhouse surrounded by barns and meadows with cattle and crops. An orchard stood nearby under a bright sky with perfect clouds.

He stood back to the enthusiastic applause of his audience, but did not put down his brush.

Instead, he began to apply darker colors in a reckless fashion canceling out the sunny sky, the tranquil meadows, and the pristine cottage. The puzzled audience remained silent this time when he laid down his brushes with a satisfied look before stepping aside to reveal a messy scene of dark tones with no order or beauty.

After a moment, Nast requested that the attendants place a gilded frame around the ruined artwork. Then he asked them to turn the framed canvas to an upright position.

The Mystery of the Gospel | Colossians 1:24-29

The audience burst into hearty ovation. By simply turning the painting, the mystery was revealed. A waterfall plunged over dark rocks in a forest of glorious trees.

This story represents the story of the whole world. It started out as a perfect home. But when sin entered the world the dark strokes of sorrow and death began to ruin the perfection God created. Even the Son of God was put to death on a Roman cross.

So often we are confused, and wonder what is going on in the world around us. But God guides even the darkest strokes that they might work His purposes. Through His Word He turns the picture, as it were, and reveals to us the mystery of the hope of the gospel through salvation in Jesus Christ.

Colossians 1:24-29 speaks of this mystery which God has revealed.

OBSERVATION

1 PRAY

Pray before reading and studying this passage that the Lord will give you understanding and wisdom through it and challenge your thinking so that you might become more like Him.

2 READ FOCUS VERSES

Read Colossians 1:24-29 and notice the different ways Paul speaks of the gospel of salvation through Jesus Christ.

3 MATCHING

Paul rejoices in — His sufferings

Christ's body — A minister or servant

Paul defines himself as — The rich glories of the mystery

The mystery hidden but now revealed — The church

What God wants His people to know — Christ living in His people

4 WHY?

Why does verse 25 explain that Paul was made a minister or servant of the gospel?

The Mystery of the Gospel | Colossians 1:24-29

5 | MINISTER

Sometimes we use the word *minister* (G1249 – diakonos) as a title without considering that it means servant, attendant, or one who obeys the commands of another.

6 | KEYWORD – MYSTERY

The mystery is the theme of this passage as it is explained and expanded on. Using a question mark ("**?**") to mark the word *mystery* both times it appears in this passage will help it stand out to you as you read.

Visit **http://ibible.study/worksheet**
to print out a Bible Worksheet for this study.

7 | MYSTERY REVEALED

How is the mystery defined at the end of verse 27?

The hope of glory in _____

The Mystery of the Gospel | Colossians 1:24-29

8 COMMISSION

What are those who know this mystery to do with it, according to verse 28? Why?

9 STRIVING

What motivated Paul to labor and strive to share the gospel?
- ○ Positive responses motivate him
- ○ He receives power from God
- ○ Others encourage him
- ○ He uses all the strength he has

The Mystery of the Gospel | Colossians 1:24-29

INTERPRETATION

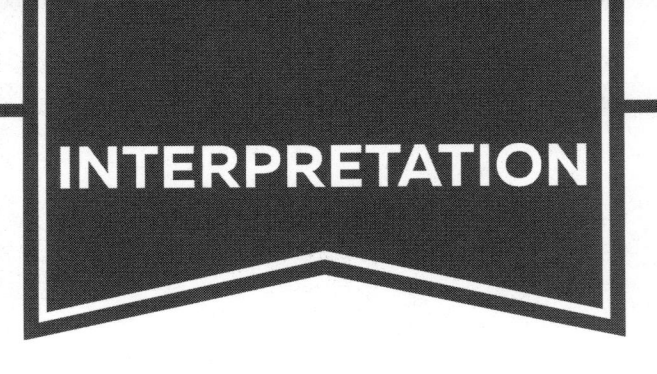

1 REJOICING

James 1:2–4 explains why a believer can rejoice in sufferings.

2 SUFFERINGS

From what we've seen in Colossians and James, why did Paul rejoice in his sufferings for Christ's sake?

The Mystery of the Gospel | Colossians 1:24–29

3 — CROSS REFERENCING

Ephesians 3:1-13 is very similar to today's passage. Read it to better understand some of the key concepts in both passages.

4 — PARALLELS

What are some of the parallels between these two sections of Scripture?

5 MANIFOLD WISDOM OF GOD

In Colossians 1:26 we read about God's mystery being revealed. Why did God reveal the mystery of the gospel, according to Ephesians 3:9-10?

6 REVEALER

In both of these passages, who had to reveal the mystery of the gospel?

- ○ Paul
- ○ No one
- ○ Any one
- ○ God

The Mystery of the Gospel | Colossians 1:24-29

7. RICHES OF HIS GLORY

In verse 27 of today's passage, we read about the riches of the glory of this mystery. The phrase is used several times in the Bible. Notice it in Philippians 4:19.

8. MYSTERY

The word *mystery* is commonly used in a few different senses. Perhaps the word even brings to mind a detective story. But unlike those mysteries, we can't figure out God's mystery on our own. The word translated *mystery* (G3466 – mystērion) in today's passage refers to something that is secret or hidden until God reveals it.

9. CHRIST IN YOU

Colossians 1:27 speaks of Christ in believers. Jesus promised this in the Gospels, and we see it throughout the New Testament. Galatians 2:20 relates this glorious reality to a Christian's daily life.

10 — INDWELLING

How would you explain these verses about Christ living in believers in your own words?

11 — HOPE OF GLORY

This is not the first time the book of Colossians has talked about hope. Glance back at chapter 1:3-5.

The Mystery of the Gospel | Colossians 1:24-29

12 HOPE

What is a Christian's certain hope?

---

13 EVERYONE

There is no one with whom a Christian should not share the hope of the gospel (verses 27–28).

○ True
○ False

The Mystery of the Gospel | Colossians 1:24–29

14 | WHO

Who is working through Paul in verse 29 to labor to share the hope of the gospel with everyone?

15 | LABOR

Paul speaks of laboring. See what he says about those labors in 1 Corinthians 15:58.

16 PROMISE

What is the promise in this verse to everyone who labors to share the hope of the gospel?

The Mystery of the Gospel | Colossians 1:24–29

APPLICATION

1 — BELIEVE

Do you believe the mystery of the gospel which God has revealed through His Word that you can receive forgiveness and salvation through the life, death, and resurrection of Jesus Christ? Why or why not?

The Mystery of the Gospel | Colossians 1:24-29

2 LABOR

If you believe the hope of the glorious mystery of God in the gospel, what are you doing, or what will you be doing, to labor to share it with everyone?

The Mystery of the Gospel | Colossians 1:24-29

CLOSING

We hope this study has helped you better understand the mystery of the gospel of Jesus Christ and challenged you to share it through His power.

JOURNAL

Write down any additional thoughts that come to mind as a result of this lesson.

The Mystery of the Gospel | Colossians 1:24-29

Additional RESOURCES

To aid in your study of this passage, we've placed the following additional resource on our website:

The Mysteries of God – This short post summarizes much of what the New Testament says about the mysteries which had been hidden but which God has now revealed.

Visit http://ibible.study/resources

The Minister's ROLE

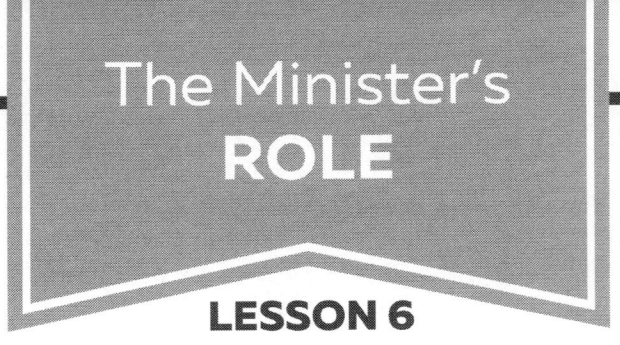

LESSON 6

BIG IDEA

Faithful Christian leaders battle for the spiritual growth of those they serve.

PASSAGE

Colossians 2:1-5

TOPIC

Christian Life

INTRODUCTION

In the mid-nineteenth century, Korea was closed to foreigners on pain of death. But Robert Thomas felt that even a closed border should not keep out the gospel. Once he had tried to visit Korea without success. But a year later, he heard of an American who planned to take an exploratory voyage to Korea.

After he had persuaded the explorers to allow him to accompany them on their dangerous voyage, Thomas brought aboard a cargo of Bibles and gospel tracts. Along the route, he gave copies of the Bible to those brave enough to receive them and left extra copies where others might find them privately.

After a visit to Pyongyang City, the ship was caught by low tides. It was set ablaze, and the men were forced to swim to shore to face a hostile crowd. According to the stories Koreans later told, all of the men emerged from the water with weapons ready for battle except one who seemed very strange.

Rather than bring weapons, this man thrust a pile of books into the hands of his attackers as they clubbed him down.

Officials sent to all the places the intruders had been to collect and burn the Bibles Thomas had left in his wake and at his death, but many copies were concealed by owners who read and treasured them. One of the first men who professed faith in Christ after missionaries were allowed to openly enter the country was the son of a man who had received one of these Bibles from Robert Thomas.

This is not a unique story. Hundreds, even thousands of men and women have been willing to risk their lives to share the Word of God and the gospel it contains with people around the world. One of the first of these bold witnesses was the apostle Paul. He suffered beatings, shipwrecks, imprisonment, abuse, and martyrdom to tell people about the Lord Jesus Christ who died to save them. In today's study of Colossians 2:1-5 we will see Paul explain why he was willing to suffer, and why any true Christian minister lives, suffers, and dies to win and encourage God's people.

OBSERVATION

1 PRAY

Before studying this passage, take some time to talk to its Author, God, who will give you wisdom through it if you will ask in humility and obedience.

2 READ FOCUS VERSES

Today's passage is the first five verses of Colossians chapter two. These verses give us a clear picture of the role a Christian leader and minister has. Look for the aspects of this ministry in Colossians 2:1–5.

3 KEYWORD – PAUL

Paul speaks of himself many times in this short passage. Go through the passage and mark each of Paul's references to himself and his role in these believers' lives with a large *p* ("**P**"). By marking these references Paul makes to himself, you'll be reminded of their significance each time you read or reference this passage.

Visit **http://ibible.study/worksheet**
to print out a Bible Worksheet for this study.

4 I WANT YOU TO KNOW

In verse 1, Paul says he wants these believers to know about the great _____ he has for them.

5 — ANOTHER CHURCH

Which other church does Paul mention by name in verse 1?
- ○ Ephesus
- ○ Laodicea
- ○ Galatia
- ○ Pergamos

6 — PRESENT

According to verse 1, Paul has visited the Colossian church.
- ○ True
- ○ False

The Minister's Role | Colossians 2:1-5

7 | 4 THINGS

Paul lists four things he wants for these believers in verse 2. Mark the order in which they appear in the text:

- ☐ That they might have all the riches of full assurance of understanding
- ☐ That they will be knit together in love
- ☐ That they would acknowledge the mystery of God
- ☐ That their hearts will be comforted

8 | TREASURES

All the treasures of wisdom and _____ are hidden in Christ (verse 3).

9 — REMINDER

In verse 4, Paul explains why he reminded them that all wisdom and knowledge come from Christ. What is his reason?

- ○ So that they will not be tricked by ideas that sound good but undermine the gospel
- ○ So that they will believe everyone who comes to teach them
- ○ So that they will not worry about learning things
- ○ So that they will not listen to anyone who comes to teach them

10 — ABSENT

Though Paul is absent, what does he say in verse 5 about his relationship to this church?

The Minister's Role | Colossians 2:1-5

11 | REJOICING

According to verse 5, which of the following are the reasons Paul explains that he rejoices in the church at Colossae?

○ Their order

○ Their openness to new ideas

○ Their steadfast faith in Christ

○ Their spontaneity

INTERPRETATION

1. CONFLICT

Paul says he wants them to know the conflict he has for them. The word translated *conflict* or *struggle* (G73 – agōn) was used to speak of a struggle, contest, battle, or race, especially at the Greek games.

2. THEIR WORK

In 1 Thessalonians 5:12-13, Paul speaks not just of himself, but of all ministers of the gospel who labor on behalf of Christ's church.

3 | ON YOUR BEHALF

What are some practical ways a minister or Christian leader fights a warfare on behalf of God's people?

4 | FRIENDS

Many of the Epistles were written to churches that Paul had started or visited. Why does he love this Colossian church so much that he bears conflict for them though he's never visited?

5 COMFORT

In verse 2, Paul desires that the hearts of these believers will be comforted. How does he say they will be comforted?

- ○ By meeting Paul
- ○ By establishing their unique identity
- ○ By being knit together in love and the understanding of the gospel
- ○ By travelling to Laodicea to talk about Paul's sufferings for them

6 BONDS OF LOVE

A few verses after we see that love is what will knit the hearts of believers together, we learn more about love in Colossians 3:14.

7 ASSURANCE

The other way Paul desires for these believers to be comforted is that they might have full assurance of their faith. What does verse 2 say that they need to come to understand more fully to have that full assurance?

8 KNOWLEDGE

2 Peter 1:1-2 builds on the theme of blessings following a deeper knowledge and understanding of God and His Word.

9 | WISDOM AND KNOWLEDGE

Read the description of this wisdom and knowledge that are hid in Christ in Romans 11:33-36.

10 | HID TREASURE

Where does God tell us He has revealed to us these treasures of wisdom and knowledge hidden in Jesus Christ?

- ○ In our minds
- ○ In our hearts
- ○ In His Word
- ○ In His creation

The Minister's Role | Colossians 2:1-5

11 DECEIVED

Paul reminds us that wisdom and knowledge are hidden in Christ so that we will not be deceived when people try to teach us falsehood. In 2 Corinthians 11:13-15, we are further warned that these deceivers can sometimes seem like they are teaching truth.

12 TRUE VS. FALSE

If false teachers can look and sound like true messengers from God, how can we tell the difference? God gives us three main questions to test teachers and see if their message is true or false:

1. What does this teacher say about Jesus (1 John 2:22-23; 4:1-3; 2 John 1:7)?
2. Does this teacher preach the gospel of salvation by grace (Galatians 1:6-9)?
3. Does this teacher obey Scripture's practical commands (Titus 1:10-11; Romans 16:17-18; 2 Peter 2:1-3)?

Read in Matthew 7:15-20 how Jesus highlights the third test – you can judge a teacher by their actions.

13 | REJOICING

Even though Paul isn't present with these believers, he can still rejoice that the believers are in order and steadfast in their faith. Standing strong in the faith is spoken of throughout the Bible as the mark of a true believer. See the encouragement in 1 Corinthians 15:58 to be steadfast.

14 | STAND FAST

We see this exhortation repeated just a few verses later in 1 Corinthians 16:13.

15 | NO GREATER JOY

Paul's joy is summarized in 3 John 1:4.

16 | GREATEST JOY

What is the best way to bring joy to a godly leader and minister?

17 | SUMMARY

How would you summarize what this passage has said about the role a leader or minister has in a Christian's life?

APPLICATION

1 — ENCOURAGER

How should your life change so that you are an encouragement and joy to the Christian leaders who minister to you?

2 — FINDING TREASURE

How are you going to prioritize knowing the Word of God so that you can find the hidden treasures of God's wisdom and knowledge in Jesus Christ?

The Minister's Role | Colossians 2:1-5

3 | STANDING FAST

If you are a believer and Paul was to write a letter to you today, could he rejoice that you are standing fast in the faith? How does your answer challenge you to grow in your Christian life?

CLOSING

We hope this study has helped you better understand the role of Christian leaders and ministers in the Christian life and challenged you to encourage the Christian leaders around you.

JOURNAL

Write down any additional thoughts that come to mind as a result of this lesson.

The Minister's Role | Colossians 2:1-5

Additional RESOURCES

To aid in your study of this passage, we've placed the following additional resource on our website:

True and False Teachers – Here is a brief summary of the ways the Bible teaches us to identify true and false teachers.

Visit http://ibible.study/resources

Who Jesus Christ Is to A BELIEVER

LESSON 7

BIG IDEA

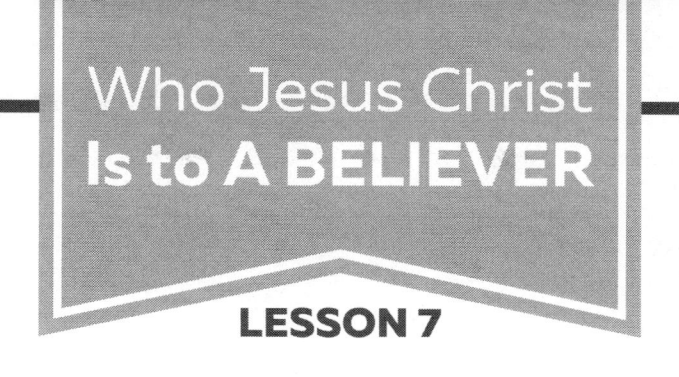

Jesus Christ is everything to those who trust in Him, so they must walk with Him and beware of those who would deceive them.

PASSAGE

Colossians 2:6–10

TOPIC

Jesus Christ

INTRODUCTION

There is a story of a Persian king who ruled in magnificent style, yet liked to disguise himself and spend time with his people. Once when he had dressed as if he was poor, he descended to a damp cellar where a lonely man seated on a pile of ashes was loading coal into a furnace.

The king sat with him while they talked. When lunch approached, the poor man shared his coarse black bread and stale water with his companion. Time and again the king returned to visit this lonely man. He, in turn, was so grateful for the compassion and good advice that he opened his heart completely to this friend who seemed as poor as himself.

After a while, the king decided that he would reveal his true position and see what the man would request from him. He explained that though he appeared poor, he was the great king.

Instead of the expected petition, the poor man looked with wonder and love on his king. At last the king spoke, "Don't you understand? I can make you wealthy or powerful with a word. Do you not have anything to ask?"

Gently the man replied, "Yes, my king, I understand. But what you have done to leave your place of glory and sit with me in this dark place, to share in my course meals, and to care whether I am happy or sad – even you can grant me nothing more precious. Others you have given rich presents, but to me you have given yourself. I only ask that you never withdraw this gift of your friendship."

This story is a little picture of what it means that the Son of God, equal to the Father in glory and power, became a man and lived, ate, slept, worked, suffered, and died like us. He didn't just give us His rich gifts, though He has bestowed those on us abundantly. He went far beyond that and gave us Himself.

Colossians 2:6-10 speaks of the relationship Christ offers to us.

OBSERVATION

1 PRAY

Before reading this passage, pray to its Author and Subject, Jesus Christ, who is God and yet desires to help you understand Himself and how you are to relate to Him.

2 READ FOCUS VERSES

Today's passage, Colossians 2:6-10, is short but holds so many important truths. As you read, identify the person to whom everything in these verses points.

3 THE CENTER

Who is the center of this passage to whom everything else points?
- ○ Paul
- ○ The church's pastor
- ○ Jesus
- ○ Moses

4 TITLES

What of these titles and names is NOT used for our Savior in this passage?

- ○ Christ
- ○ Jesus
- ○ Lord
- ○ Son

5 KEYWORD – JESUS CHRIST

Mark with a cross ("✝") all of the titles, names, and pronouns (like *He, Him, His*) that refer to Jesus Christ in Colossians 2:6-10.

Visit **http://ibible.study/worksheet** to print out a Bible Worksheet for this study.

6 TO WHOM

In verse 6, we see what defines the people to whom this passage is addressed. What word is used to describe the way they have responded to Jesus Christ?

They have _____ Him.

7 NOW WHAT

In your own words, what two things do verses 6-8 tell these people, who have received Christ as Lord, to do?

1. _____

2. _____

Who Jesus Christ Is to a Believer | Colossians 2:6-10

8 | WHY?

According to verses 9-10, why do verses 6-8 command Christians to follow Jesus Christ and beware of false teaching?

9 | OVERFLOWING

What are Christians supposed to overflow with, according to verse 7?

- ○ Thanksgiving
- ○ Love
- ○ Joy
- ○ Hope

10 KEYWORD – BEWARE!

There is a very strong warning in verse 8. Use a triangle with an exclamation mark in the center ("⚠") to visually emphasize the importance of this warning.

Visit **http://ibible.study/worksheet**
to print out a Bible Worksheet for this study.

11 BE VERY CAREFUL

What does verse 8 warn Christians to be careful of?

Who Jesus Christ Is to a Believer | Colossians 2:6–10

12 MATCHING

Dwells in Jesus Christ ●   ● Christ

Believers are complete in ●   ● All principality and power

Christ is head over ●   ● The fullness of God's nature

INTERPRETATION

1. RECEIVING CHRIST

John 1:12–13 also speaks of receiving Christ. Notice how it speaks of those who have received Him.

2. EXPLAIN

To receive Christ you must believe on His _____, according to John 1:12–13.

3. FOLLOWING

Read 1 John 2:6 and consider how it relates to the command in Colossians 2:6.

4 | SO WALK

According to 1 John 2:6, how does a true Christian live?

5 | ESTABLISHED

Colossians 2:7 sounds similar to 1:21–23.

6 | IMPORTANT

Why is it important for a believer to be established in Christ and not move away from Him?

7 › WITH THANKSGIVING

There are so many passages in Scripture that speak about giving thanks, like verse 7 in today's passage. Let's look at two beginning in Colossians 3:15-17.

8 › GIVE THANKS

Notice that 1 Thessalonians 5:18 also speaks of giving thanks.

9 › HOW MUCH

Based on what we've see in these verses, how would you describe how important it is for a Christian to give thanks and how much they should be thankful?

Who Jesus Christ Is to a Believer | Colossians 2:6-10

10 ROBBED

In verse 8, Christians are warned not to let the world spoil them of their rewards through deceit. The word translated *spoil* or *take captive* (G4812 – sylagōgeō) speaks of taking away booty, taking someone captive, or seducing someone away from the truth.

11 PHILOSOPHIES

God summarizes the world's deceitful philosophy which is used to rob Christians in 1 John 2:15-17.

12 OPPOSED

Why can a believer not accept both Christ and the philosophies of the world?

13 THE GODHEAD

Verse 9 expresses the marvelous truth that Jesus Christ is fully God even though He is fully man. In His human body He is still the fullness of God. Jesus, who is as fully God as God the Father, entered our world and took a human body to reveal God to us and to save us from our sins. Why is it important that Jesus Christ is both God and man?

14 COMPLETE IN CHRIST

Scripture uses the phrase *in Christ* many times. Those two words represent so many wonderful truths. In Christ, Christians are chosen, loved, redeemed, forgiven, justified, adopted, and more. How would you describe what it means to be "in Christ" to a new believer?

Who Jesus Christ Is to a Believer | Colossians 2:6–10

15 — WHAT A FRIEND!

In Jesus, Christians have everything and more. Pause to worship Him with the familiar lyrics of "What a Friend We Have in Jesus."

> What a Friend we have in Jesus,
> All our sins and griefs to bear!
> What a privilege to carry
> Everything to God in prayer!
> O what peace we often forfeit,
> O what needless pain we bear,
> All because we do not carry
> Everything to God in prayer!
>
> Have we trials and temptations?
> Is there trouble anywhere?
> We should never be discouraged,
> Take it to the Lord in prayer.
> Can we find a friend so faithful
> Who will all our sorrows share?
> Jesus knows our every weakness,
> Take it to the Lord in prayer.

Are we weak and heavy-laden,
Cumbered with a load of care?
Precious Savior, still our refuge –
Take it to the Lord in prayer;
Do thy friends despise, forsake thee?
Take it to the Lord in prayer;
In His arms He'll take and shield thee,
Thou wilt find a solace there.

Joseph Scriven

APPLICATION

1 — RECEIVING CHRIST

Have you received Jesus Christ as Lord by believing in His Name and everything He says about Himself and accepting His sacrifice on your behalf for eternal salvation? How do you know?

2 — HAVE YOU BEEN ROBBED?

If you have received Christ, have you let something rob you of reward by deceiving you with the philosophies and ideas of this world? How will you get back to Jesus Christ and walk with Him today?

Who Jesus Christ Is to a Believer | Colossians 2:6-10

CLOSING

We hope this study has helped you understand what Jesus Christ is in a believer's life, and challenged you to prepare yourself so you won't be deceived.

JOURNAL

Write down any additional thoughts that come to mind as a result of this lesson.

Additional RESOURCES

To aid in your study of this passage, we've placed the following additional resources on our website:

The Mysteries of God – This short post explains how other verses in Scripture shed light on the marvelous truth of verse 9 that Jesus Christ is fully God and yet fully man.

Complete – Verse 10 reminds us that those who have received Christ are complete in Him. Read these thirteen things Scripture tells us that it means for a Christian to be "in Christ."

What a Friend! – Listen to this wonderful hymn and reflect on who Jesus is.

Visit http://ibible.study/resources

The 4 Ways Christians Have VICTORY OVER SIN

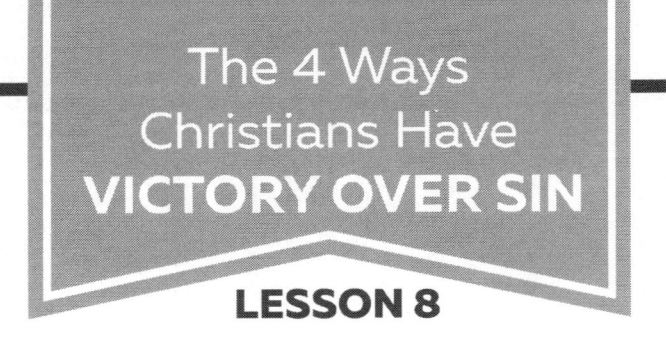

LESSON 8

BIG IDEA

By defeating sin, Christ has freed His people to live in victory.

PASSAGE

Colossians 2:11-15

TOPIC

Victory

INTRODUCTION

When the costly battle of Iwo Jima was won, there were still nearly 3,000 Japanese troops on the island. The island was won, there was no possibility of Allied defeat, yet the fighting continued for days. In fact, the last Japanese soldier didn't surrender until six years after the victory.

This is a small picture of a wonderful spiritual reality. When Jesus Christ died on the cross and then rose again, He defeated Satan, sin, and death – completely. The war is won. There is no possibility of a reversal.

Yet we continue to fight temptation until Jesus returns. Sometimes it feels like things go back and forth. When we look at the big picture, though, we realize that we are only moving toward a finished victory.

Colossians 2:11-15 speaks of this reality and the four ways a Christian has victory over sin through Christ. Remembering that sin's defeat is certain will give you power in your fight against sin because, if you are a Christian, you have won, will win, and you can't lose. Learn more about this glorious reality from Colossians.

OBSERVATION

1 — PRAY

Before studying this encouraging passage, pray and ask God to help you understand it not only for others, but for yourself and your own life.

2 — READ FOCUS VERSES

Read Colossians 2:11-15 and see what it says about a Christian's relationship to sin.

3 — CONTEXT

Read these verses in the context of verses 8-15 to see more about how the nature of Christ impacts the truths of this passage.

4 CIRCUMCISION

What does this spiritual circumcision without hands do in a believer's life?

Takes away the power of the _____

5 MATCHING

Picture of being buried and rising with Christ (v. 12)   ○   ○ Baptism

What God does when He forgives a person (v. 13)   ○   ○ Rulers of darkness

Blotted out (v. 14)   ○   ○ Makes them alive

Jesus made an open, triumphant show of (v. 15)   ○   ○ The record of sin

The 4 Ways Christians Have Victory over Sin | Colossians 2:11–15

6) HOW?

What did God do with that record of sin and its debt such that it is cancelled?

- ◯ Burned it
- ◯ Nailed it to Christ's cross
- ◯ Threw it away
- ◯ Rewrote it in heaven

7) KEYWORDS – SIN AND FLESH

You can see that the words denoting sin and the flesh are critical to understanding Colossians 2:11-15. By putting a large *x* ("**X**") over these words, they'll stand out to you as you consider a Christian's relationship to sin because Christ has defeated it.

Visit **http://ibible.study/worksheet**
to print out a Bible Worksheet for this study.

INTERPRETATION

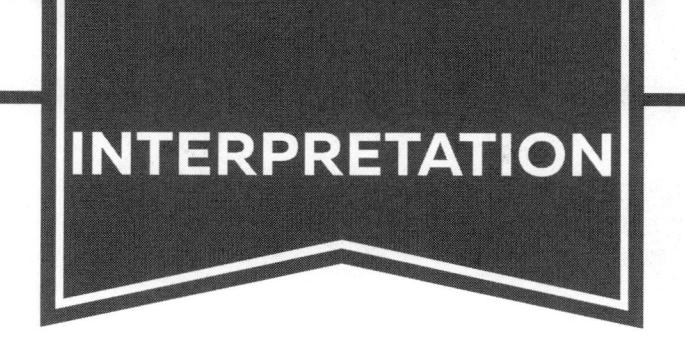

1 STRUCTURE

This passage is written with the results first and the reason last, so let's begin at the heart of the passage and work our way to the response we should have. Who is it that wins this victory for Christians?

- ○ The Christian him or herself
- ○ The conflict goes away on its own
- ○ Satan concedes
- ○ Christ won through the cross

2 BLOTTING OUT

The Bible speaks many times of records being blotted out – completely obliterated. Notice the parallel between Isaiah 44:22 and Colossians 2:14.

3. NAILED TO HIS CROSS

Verse 14 speaks of the record of our sins being nailed to Christ's cross. Reflect on this glorious thought expressed in the middle verse of "It Is Well with My Soul."

> My sin – oh, the bliss of this glorious thought –
> My sin, not in part, but the whole,
> Is nailed to His Cross, and I bear it no more;
> Praise the Lord, praise the Lord, O my soul!
> It is well, it is well with my soul!
>
> Horatio Gates Spafford

4. THE ENEMY

We are introduced to the same enemy mentioned in Colossians 2:15 in Ephesians 6:12.

5. NO POWER

Notice what Romans 8:38-39 says about the powerlessness of these dark enemies.

6 · AN OPEN SHOW

When a Roman general would return from victory, he would bring the captured army's generals with him. They would be displayed as part of his homecoming parade to show the Roman citizens that the enemy had been completely vanquished. Why is that picture used for what Jesus Christ did to the world, the flesh, and the devil which He conquered on our behalf?

7 · SIN'S WAGES

To better understand the power of verse 14, read Romans 6:23.

8 | HIS CROSS

Why did Jesus Christ have to die to pay the debts we owe so that they could be blotted out?

9 | BAPTISM

Verse 12 in today's passage speaks of the picture of baptism. It symbolizes a Christian's relationship to the death and resurrection of Jesus Christ and His victory over sin and death. Romans 6 expands on this theme. Read Romans 6:3-12.

10 | SYMBOLIZE

How does baptism symbolize a Christian's relationship to sin through Christ?

11 RISEN

Romans 6 emphasizes that through Christ's death and resurrection a Christian is dead to sin and alive to serving God. Colossians 3 speaks of the same theme. Read Colossians 3:1-4 to see the beginning of this thought.

12 MINDSET

On what is a Christian's mind to be set?
- ○ Things above
- ○ The present
- ○ Things of earth
- ○ The past

The 4 Ways Christians Have Victory over Sin | Colossians 2:11-15

13 CIRCUMCISION

In Genesis, God commanded Abraham that all the Israelite men were to be circumcised as a sign of the covenant. God's covenant with Israel made them His special people. But not everyone who was physically circumcised as a Jew was a believer with eternal salvation. So, in Deuteronomy 30:6 God promised that one day He would circumcise their hearts spiritually by cutting away the sinful flesh. Read that verse to see the promise yourself.

14 RESULTS

According to this verse in Deuteronomy, what is the result in someone's life when God takes away the old nature?

15 | IN YOUR OWN WORDS

You've seen that a believer has victory over sin in four ways:
1. Christ's conquest on the cross
2. Being dead to sin in Christ
3. Having new life through Christ's resurrection
4. Putting off the old man and having the heart purified.

How would you explain this passage to someone who asked you what it meant?

The 4 Ways Christians Have Victory over Sin | Colossians 2:11-15

APPLICATION

1 ARE YOU SURE

Are you so sure that your sins have been blotted out and that you are free from the power of death and sin, that you can say "it is well with my soul" no matter what is happening around you? Is there something in your life that needs to change?

2 LIVING FREE

If you are a Christian, in what ways do you need to begin to live like sin is defeated and you have conquered it through Christ?

CLOSING

We hope this study has helped you understand four ways Christ has defeated sin and how that frees His people to live in victory.

JOURNAL

Write down any additional thoughts that come to mind as a result of this lesson.

The 4 Ways Christians Have Victory over Sin | Colossians 2:11-15

Additional RESOURCES

To aid in your study of this passage, we've placed the following additional resource on our website:

It Is Well – Listen to the beautiful hymn "It Is Well" and be reminded of what Jesus Christ has done for you.

Visit http://ibible.study/resources

The True Freedom OF A CHRISTIAN

LESSON 9

BIG IDEA

A Christian is free from sin and the Law to live for Christ.

PASSAGE

Colossians 2:16–23

TOPIC

Freedom

INTRODUCTION

Over four centuries ago, a young monk named Martin Luther was zealously seeking peace with God. He followed every rule of his monastery, and punished his body through starvation, beatings, and hard labor. He was striving to kill his sin nature and earn God's favor. Sometimes in his zeal, he brought himself very near death. Others were concerned for him, and yet he was willing to lose his life if somehow he could find peace for his soul.

His superiors tried to distract him with education and responsibility hoping he would mellow with age, but still he could find nothing to satisfy his soul or free him from the chains of sin.

Nothing, that is, until he read in Romans that "the just shall live by faith." All of his knowledge of Scripture came rushing back as the Holy Spirit gave him understanding. Finally he grasped the reality that he could never pay for his own sins or remove their power through any works of his own. All the rules and regulations he could impose on himself could not make him acceptable to God.

By faith he must believe that Jesus Christ by His death had paid for Luther's sins – and would completely erase their record. Through His resurrection, Christ had conquered the power of sin and the Law. Now there was freedom!

When he saw this the light of heaven burst upon his troubled soul. Suddenly he understood that we only "have peace with God through our Lord Jesus Christ." And it is Christ's perfect life, death, and resurrection that free us from sin and the Law to live in loving obedience to God.

Colossians 2:16-23 speaks of this freedom in Christ. The rules and regulations cannot free us from sin or its power. Instead, through the death of Christ a Christian is free from them to live for God and be at peace with Him.

OBSERVATION

1 PRAY

Before reading this passage, pray that God will teach you to understand what it means and help you reject anything false you have believed or been taught that disagrees with what Scripture says.

2 READ FOCUS VERSES

As you read Colossians 2:16-23 notice all the things from which a Christian is free.

3 THEREFORE

You probably noticed that this passage starts off with a "therefore" phrase which means the truths of this passage are based on the truths of the last one. Read Colossians 2:8-23 to understand the present passage.

The True Freedom of a Christian | Colossians 2:16-23

4 FOUNDATION

How would you summarize the truths in Colossians 2:11-15 which lead up to today's verses?

5 JUDGE

What is a Christian not supposed to allow in verse 16?

Let no one _____ them about certain observances

6 WHY?

Why is a Christian not to allow others to judge what they do or don't do in regard to certain things in Moses' Law, according to verse 17?

- ○ Those things were a shadow pointing to Jesus Christ
- ○ It doesn't matter to God what we do or don't do
- ○ It isn't anyone's business what we do or don't do

The True Freedom of a Christian | Colossians 2:16-23

7 MATCHING

A Christian can be tricked to lose (v.18) ○   ○ They are dead with Christ to the world

A Christian can never worship (v.18) ○   ○ Their reward

Why a Christian is free from these observances (v.20) ○   ○ Angels

8 HOLDING FAST

According to verse 19, what is a Christian to do instead of these other things from which he or she is free?

○ Live as they please

○ Hold fast to Christ

○ Flaunt their liberty

The True Freedom of a Christian | Colossians 2:16-23

9 FREED

When a person dies with Christ, what do verses 20-21 say they are freed from?

The commands and teachings of _____

10 A SHOW

In your own words, how would you summarize what verse 23 says about these false rules?

11 KEYWORD – CHRIST

Christ is the center of this passage – the reason for a Christian's freedom and the One to whom they turn because they are free. Put a cross ("✝") over all of the words naming or referring to Jesus Christ in today's passage (consider doing this for the whole chapter).

Visit **http://ibible.study/worksheet** to print out a Bible Worksheet for this study.

The True Freedom of a Christian | Colossians 2:16-23

INTERPRETATION

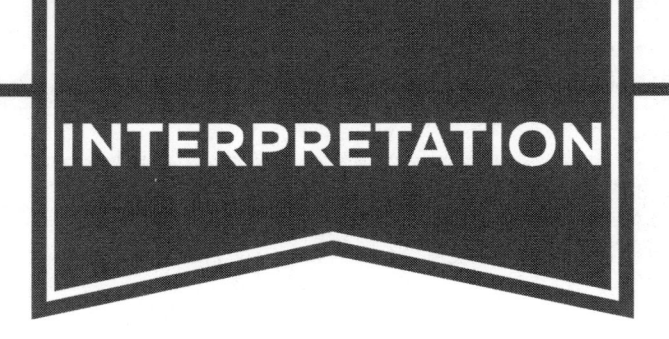

1 PASSING JUDGMENT

Think about the word translated *judge* (G2919 – krinō) in verse 16. It means to pronounce a sentence, to call into question, or to authoritatively declare whether something is right or wrong.

2 SETTING THE STANDARD

Notice that in 1 Corinthians 4:3-4 Paul goes further to say that not only can people not set the standard of what is right for others, they can't set it for themselves.

3 | WHO?

According to these verses, since a Christian cannot be ultimately judged by themselves or by others, who judges them?

[   ]

4 | THE LAW

The things listed in Colossians 2:16 are parts of the Mosaic Law given in Exodus through Deuteronomy. A believer in the Old Testament showed their faith by obeying these observances.

In verse 17, Paul explains why a Christian today is free from observing those rules of the Law by describing them as shadows pointing to a reality – Christ. Hebrews speaks extensively of the way the Law is a shadow of Christ. Notice what Hebrews 10:1 says about the Law.

5 | A SHADOW

What are some of the reasons you can think of that the Law would be called a shadow of the reality of Christ – something that indicated vaguely the reality it was representing?

6 | SET FREE

Galatians 5:1 concludes a long section explaining how Christians are free from the Mosaic Law.

7 | REWARD

Hebrews 11:6 speaks of the reward mentioned in Colossians 2:18.

The True Freedom of a Christian | Colossians 2:16-23

8 | TO WHOM?

To whom does Hebrews 11:6 say that God will give this reward?
- ◯ Everyone
- ◯ No one
- ◯ Christians
- ◯ Those who diligently seek Him

9 | WHY?

By tying these three passages together, how would you explain why a believer who is distracted by false rules will lose reward?

10 | HUMILITY

Verses 18 and 23 in today's passage both speak of a false humility. Compare this humility with the true humility described in 1 Peter 5:6.

The True Freedom of a Christian | Colossians 2:16–23

11 DIFFERENCE

How can you tell the difference between true and false humility?

12 VICTORY

Verses 20-23 speak of regulations which punish the body but do not protect from temptation. In the following quotes, Thomas Chalmers explains what actually will overcome temptation to sin:

"The best way to overcome the world is not with morality or self-discipline. Christians overcome the world by seeing the beauty and excellence of Christ. They overcome the world by seeing something more attractive than the world: Christ."

"The only way to dispossess [the heart] of an old affection is by the expulsive power of a new one."

The True Freedom of a Christian | Colossians 2:16-23

13 | THE ANSWER

Since rules and morality are not the answer to overcoming temptation, what is? How would you explain the answer to a friend?

14 | NOT A COVER FOR SIN

Colossians has clearly shown that a Christian is free from the Law. Read the warning in Galatians 5:13 about this freedom.

15 | UNDER GRACE

This warning is further explained by Romans 6:12-18.

The True Freedom of a Christian | Colossians 2:16-23

16 FREEDOM

Based on these three passages in Galatians, Romans, and Colossians, what does it mean that a Christian is free. Or, in other words, what will that freedom look like and not look like?

17 CELEBRATION

Conclude with the joyful exclamation in 1 Corinthians 15:55–58 which explains how freedom from sin and the Law allows God's people to love and live for Jesus Christ.

The True Freedom of a Christian | Colossians 2:16–23

APPLICATION

1 — SET FREE

Have you been set free by putting your faith in Jesus Christ's death to pay for your sins? How do you know?

2 — LIVING FREE

In what ways are you living the kind of fake freedom that imposes worldly regulations on you and robs you of eternal reward? Instead, how can you live truly free in Christ to love and obey God?

The True Freedom of a Christian | Colossians 2:16–23

CLOSING

We hope this study has helped you understand how a Christian is truly free from sin and the Law to live for Christ.

JOURNAL

Write down any additional thoughts that come to mind as a result of this lesson.

What Does It Look Like to Be Risen WITH CHRIST?

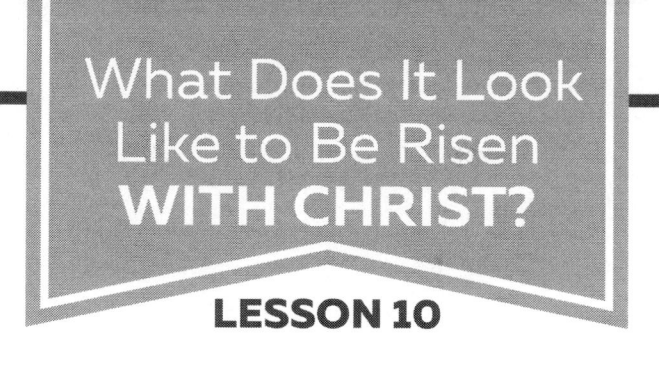

LESSON 10

BIG IDEA

When a Christian understands what it means that they are risen with Christ, it radically changes what they love and how they live.

PASSAGE

Colossians 3:1-4

TOPIC

Christian Life

INTRODUCTION

A little girl received a letter from the King. It told her that He had adopted her as His daughter. She was to journey to the palace which was now her home. He had written specific instructions for her to follow along the way.

Most of her neighbors laughed when they saw it. They took it as nothing more than a practical joke. When they saw that she believed it and planned to act on its instructions, they mocked her and sought to dissuade her. Nothing the new princess could say would convince her neighbors or show them why she believed the King's missive. But she had full faith in her King and began her journey.

You can imagine her carefully studying and following His instructions along the way. Nothing – candy, toys, comforts – could distract her from her goal. Once a merchant tried to woo her away from her journey with a promise of fine clothes. With polite firmness she told him that she was to have much finer clothes soon.

She just kept on her way, looking straight ahead to her life to come. This constant focus on her new identity and home encouraged her and gave her strength to press on.

You too have received an invitation from the King of the universe. He sent His Son to pay the debt for all of your sin so that you could be accepted in God's sight. He desires to adopt you, to make you His child and heir of all He possesses. He has given you His Word to guide your path and show you how to live. He has given you His Holy Spirit to be your Guide and Comforter.

Colossians 3:1-4 speaks of how this reality shapes a Christian's life. Those who believe God's gift of life will live for and love heaven and the Savior who died and rose again to make it theirs.

OBSERVATION

1 | PRAY

Before reading and studying this passage of the Bible, pray and ask God to give you wisdom, convict you, encourage you, and direct you through it.

2 | READ FOCUS VERSES

Today's passage may be short, but it is full of glorious truth. Read Colossians 3:1-4 and see if you can pick out the theme of these verses.

3 | KEYWORD – RISEN

Though it only appears once in these verses, you probably noticed that the word *risen* is a keyword around which the whole passage revolves. Use an up arrow ("↑") to mark this word and highlight its significance in Colossians 3:1-4.

Visit **http://ibible.study/worksheet** to print out a Bible Worksheet for this study.

4 | WHO?

How does verse 1 define the people to whom these verses are addressed?

- ○ Dead to sin
- ○ Alive to hope
- ○ Risen with Christ
- ○ Adopted by love

5 | WHO?

What two things are people who are risen with Christ to do as commanded in verses 1 and 2?

_____ and set your _____ on the things that are above.

What Does It Look Like to Be Risen with Christ? | Colossians 3:1-4

6 WHO?

His presence defines "above" (v. 1) ○　　○ Things on the earth

A believer should not set their ○　　○ A Christian's life
affection on (v. 2)

Christ is (v. 4) ○　　○ Christ

7 HOW?

How does verse 3 explain the commands that God's people should look for and love things above and not on the earth?

What Does It Look Like to Be Risen with Christ? | Colossians 3:1-4

8 | APPEAR

What will happen when Christ appears, according to verse 4?

What Does It Look Like to Be Risen with Christ? | Colossians 3:1-4

INTERPRETATION

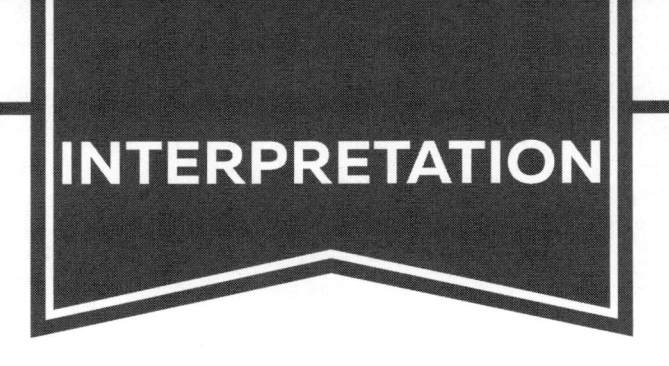

1. MADE ALIVE

Ephesians 2:4-9 speaks of the way a person is raised with Christ.

2. HOW DO YOU KNOW?

How does someone know if they are risen with Christ?

3. IF NOT

If you have not accepted Christ's free gift of salvation and been raised with Him, Romans 10:9-13 explains how.

What Does It Look Like to Be Risen with Christ? | Colossians 3:1-4

4 | SEEK

In Matthew 6:25-34, Jesus explains what it means to seek those things which are above.

5 | I SPY

What will seeking things above look like in a person's life? What are some ways you could identify someone who is living for heaven?

6 | AFFECTION

The second command in today's passage is that a believer set their love on things above not things on the earth. Jesus explains what this will look like in Matthew 6:19-24.

What Does It Look Like to Be Risen with Christ? | Colossians 3:1-4

7 | IN YOUR OWN WORDS

In your own words, how would you summarize these passages in Matthew and Colossians and what they mean for your life?

8 | GOD'S RIGHT HAND

Many times in Scripture we are told that Jesus Christ sat down on the right hand of God. Hebrews 12:1-2 is especially beautiful.

9 | CHRIST LIVES IN ME

Consider what Paul says in Galatians 2:20.

10 | CHRIST = LIFE

What are some aspects of what it means that Christ is a Christian's life?

11 | APPEAR

1 Thessalonians 4:13-18 further explains what it means for Christ to appear.

12 | WITH ME

In John 14:1-6, Jesus speaks of believers being with Him in glory.

13 | LIKE HIM

As we see in 1 John 3:2, Christians will not only be with Christ, but also be like Him.

What Does It Look Like to Be Risen with Christ? | Colossians 3:1-4

14 UNDERSTANDING

How would you explain Colossians 3:4 in light of these other passages?

15 LOOKING FOR IT

Just like Colossians 3, Titus 2:11-14 speaks of how hoping for Christ's appearing changes a Christian's life.

16 STRANGERS AND PILGRIMS

Since Christians are living for heaven, God describes them as strangers and pilgrims on earth in 1 Peter 2:11-12.

APPLICATION

1 — LIVING FOR HEAVEN

How are you going to set your love and heart on things above – laying up treasure in heaven – today? What will that look like in your life?

2 — PILGRIMS ON EARTH

What will it look like today for you not to love and seek the things of this earth, but to live as a traveler passing through to the place Christ has prepared?

CLOSING

We hope this study has helped you understand how Christ's resurrection changes what a Christian loves and how they live.

JOURNAL

Write down any additional thoughts that come to mind as a result of this lesson.

Additional RESOURCES

To aid in your study of this passage, we've placed the following additional resource on our website:

Not My Home – The simple gospel song "This World Is Not My Home" reflects on the realities spoken of in Colossians 3:1-4.

Visit http://ibible.study/resources

How a Christian TREATS SIN

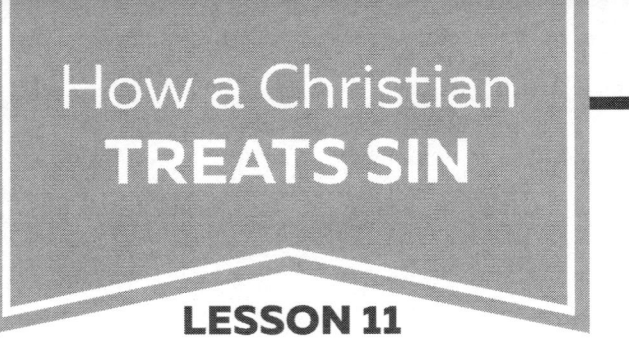

LESSON 11

BIG IDEA

A Christian seeks to destroy the sin in their life and puts it off like dirty clothes.

PASSAGE

Colossians 3:5-8

TOPIC

Sin

INTRODUCTION

Can you imagine being a 12-year-old boy and being invited to go hunting with the men of your small town? For Jimmy it was exhilarating. He couldn't wait to go be one of the men finding food for their hungry families.

Part way through the morning, one of the men told Jimmy to look for game in a hole by a tree. No sooner had Jimmy bent down to examine the hole than a skunk appeared, wheeled about, and let it loose. He had been tricked!

There was nothing he could do about it now. He smelled awful – a kind of awful he knew wouldn't go away for days, maybe weeks.

When he got home, Jimmy's mom wouldn't let him near the house. She even made him burn his clothes – the only way they knew to rid them of their foul aroma.

If you were sprayed by a skunk, would you keep the clothes around and wear them as a memory? Not likely. You would take them off as fast as possible and get rid of them.

How a Christian Treats Sin | Colossians 3:5-8

Putting off filthy clothes is one of the pictures used in Colossians 3:5-8 to describe a Christian's relationship to sin. Now that he or she has found life in Jesus Christ, they will put off the 'clothes' of sin. Dive in to understand more about what a Christian puts off and what that means.

OBSERVATION

1 PRAY

Before opening this passage, pray and ask God to open your eyes to truly understand it and change your life according to it.

2 READ FOCUS VERSES

Read Colossians 3:5-8, the verses we'll be studying today.

3 A LITTLE CONTEXT

Colossians 3:1-4 gives the context for understanding why verses 5-8 say what they do. Read Colossians 3:1-8 to understand the passage better.

4 | AUDIENCE

To whom are these verses primarily addressed?
- ⭘ Everyone
- ⭘ Christians
- ⭘ Unbelievers
- ⭘ Epaphras

5 | THEREFORE

Verse 5 opens "therefore." This means that the truths in this passage are dependent on the truths which came before them. What truths were presented in verses 1-4 which help us understand verses 5-8?

6) KEYWORDS – KILL AND TAKE OFF

Verses 5 and 8 both command Christians to take certain action concerning sin. Use an up arrow with double strikethrough ("⧧") to mark both of these words that explain a Christian's proper relationship to sin.

Visit **http://ibible.study/worksheet**
to print out a Bible Worksheet for this study.

7) KEYWORDS – SINS

Colossians 3:5-8 lists a lot of sins that a Christian is to kill and put off. Mark these with a large *x* ("**X**") for further notice and study.

8) COVETOUSNESS

At its root, God says covetousness is _____ (verse 5).

9 | BECAUSE OF

According to verse 6, what happens to people because of sin?
- ○ They get sick
- ○ God is unhappy
- ○ They are dissatisfied
- ○ God sends His wrath on them

10 | ONCE UPON A TIME

In your own words, what does verse 7 say?

How a Christian Treats Sin | Colossians 3:5-8

INTERPRETATION

1 MORTIFY

Look at the word translated *mortify* or *put to death* (G3499 – nekroō) which is used in verse 5 to tell Christians to kill their sinful desires and habits. It means to slay, to destroy the strength of, to put to death.

2 PUT OFF

Now look at the word translated *put off* or *put away* (G659 – apotithēmi) which commands Christians to put off sinful thoughts, words, and actions. It means to cast away or put off.

3 IMMORALITY

The Ten Commandments forbid adultery, and in Matthew 5:27-28 Jesus explains what God means by that – any sensual thought towards someone who is not your spouse.

4. PLEASURES FOR A MOMENT

Perhaps it seems strange that something sinful could be at all pleasurable. However, God explains in Hebrews 11:24-26 that sin has a fleeting pleasure that only lasts briefly.

5. ETERNAL PLEASURES

In contrast, notice where Psalm 16:11 says that we can find pleasures that last forever.

6. COVETOUSNESS AND IDOLATRY

Notice that Ephesians 5:5 calls covetousness idolatry just as today's passage does.

7. IDOLS

An idol is anything we love more than we love God. Idols are not always evil things. Sometimes we turn God's gifts like family, work, or possessions into idols. What makes them idols is the way we begin to shape our lives around them instead of around the Lord. God warns against having idols of the heart in Ezekiel 14:3.

8 COVETOUSNESS AND IDOLATRY

Why does God call covetousness (not being content with what you have or being stingy) idolatry?

9 A WARNING

Colossians 3:6 warns us that it is because of these sins that the wrath of God comes against those who disobey. Read how Ephesians 5:6 warns us not to listen to those who try to deceive us and say that God is not angry about sin.

10 SINNERS

Notice that Colossians 3:7 does not say Christians are people who never sin, rather they once walked in sin, but now reject sin to accept the Savior. Read about this in Ephesians 2:1-10.

11 AT ONE TIME

1 Corinthians 6:9-11 speaks of this dilemma. Christians once were people who could not inherit the kingdom of God because of their sins. Notice what verse 11 says about how God solved that problem so that His people can inherit heaven though they were once sinners too.

12 PUT IT ALL TOGETHER

Putting all these passages together, why can people who were once sinners and could not inherit heaven now be children of God with heaven as their home?

13 | THE THINGS YOU SAY

Looking at Colossians 3:8-9, what kind of things should a Christian not say?

14 | OUT OF THE HEART

In Matthew 12:34, Jesus explains where our words come from.

15 | THOUGHTS

Jesus clearly teaches us that the things we say come from our thoughts. If a Christian must not speak in certain ways, should they think those thoughts they are not to speak? Why or why not?

How a Christian Treats Sin | Colossians 3:5-8

16 SUMMARY

In your own words, summarize what a Christian is to put off and kill according to this passage in Colossians.

APPLICATION

1 | ARE YOU IN?

Have you put away sin and turned to Jesus Christ, becoming a sinner saved by grace? What are you going to do about that?

2 | COVETOUSNESS

What do you naturally covet? How are you going to deal with that now that you've seen that covetousness is idolatry?

3 THOUGHTS AND WORDS

What needs to change about your thoughts and words to submit them to the guidelines of God's will in this passage?

4 PURITY

Are there thoughts, actions, influences, friends, resources in your life that are making it hard for you to resist sexual temptations like those mentioned in verse 5? What are you going to do about it?

CLOSING

We hope this has helped you understand a Christian's relationship to sin and challenged you to destroy it and put it off.

JOURNAL

Write down any additional thoughts that come to mind as a result of this lesson.

Additional RESOURCES

To aid in your study of this passage, we've placed the following additional resource on our website:

Idolatry – Read this short and insightful discussion on how covetousness is idolatry.

Visit http://ibible.study/resources

Which Coat Will You Wear TODAY?

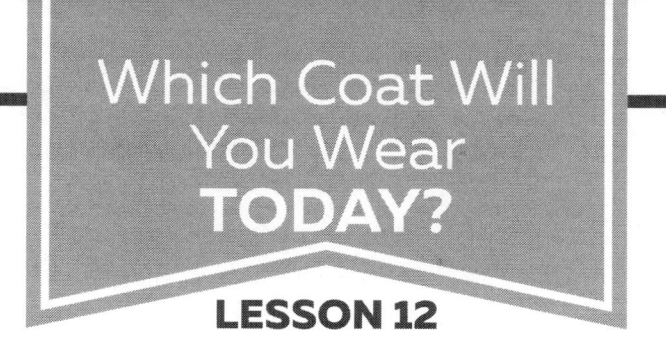

LESSON 12

BIG IDEA

Each Christian must choose to put off the old, sinful nature and put on the new, Christ-like nature.

PASSAGE

Colossians 3:9-12

TOPIC

Christian Life

INTRODUCTION

If you had a car with a bad engine and took it to the shop to have it replaced with a new one, would you expect it to run poorly on your way home? If it did, you might suspect that the shop had only cleaned the old engine.

The same is true in a Christian's life. The old, sinful nature and the new, Christ-like nature are entirely different. If there isn't much changed about your life, you would begin to wonder if your nature had been truly changed or only cleaned up.

Colossians 3:9-12 defines these two natures and gives a few examples of the difference between them. Study this passage to understand the contrast between these two natures and be challenged to put off the old one and put on the new.

OBSERVATION

1. PRAY

Before diving into this passage, pray that the Lord will open your heart and mind to understand the passage and help you live what He shows you.

2. READ FOCUS VERSES

Read Colossians 3:9-12 and notice the contrast in these verses.

3. CONTEXT

This passage is part of a longer discussion. Read Colossians 3:1-17 to get context and understand today's passage better.

4 CONTRAST

What contrast do you see in verses 9-10?

5 KEYWORD – PUT OFF AND PUT ON

Mark the key phrases *put off* and *put on* in today's passage with a clockwise arrow ("↻").

Visit **http://ibible.study/worksheet**
to print out a Bible Worksheet for this study.

Which Coat Will You Wear Today? | Colossians 3:9-12

6 | DO NOT

What does verse 9 specifically say those who have put off the old man should not do anymore?

- ○ Steal
- ○ Curse
- ○ Lie
- ○ Kill

7 | NEW MAN

How is the new man described in verse 10?

Which Coat Will You Wear Today? | Colossians 3:9-12

8 | NO DIFFERENCE

Why does verse 11 explain that God does not differentiate between people who have put on the new man?

Christ is _____ and in _____.

9 | IN CHRIST

How does verse 12 define people who are in Christ?

10 | DO THIS

What are some of the things listed in this passage that people who have put on the new man are to do?

Which Coat Will You Wear Today? | Colossians 3:9-12

INTERPRETATION

1 — OFF AND ON

The visual imagery of putting off the old nature and putting on the new one is used again in Ephesians 4:22-24.

2 — IN YOUR OWN WORDS

In your own words, what does it mean to put off the old, sinful nature and to put on the new, Christ-like nature?

3 — NO MORE LYING

One of the first visible steps of putting off the old man which is emphasized both in Colossians and Ephesians is to stop lying. Notice that Ephesians goes a step beyond that and clarifies what putting on the new man looks like in that area of life. Read Ephesians 4:25.

Which Coat Will You Wear Today? | Colossians 3:9-12

4 | NEW WAYS

What does Ephesians explain that a Christian should do now instead of lying?

5 | WHY?

Proverbs 12:22 explains why lying is unacceptable for a believer.

6 | THE IMAGE OF GOD

Both today's passage and Ephesians speak of the new nature being renewed after the image of God. If we go back to Genesis 1:26-27, we will see that people are made in the image of God.

7 | COME SHORT

Notice what Romans 3:23 says about the image of God in people.

Which Coat Will You Wear Today? | Colossians 3:9-12

8 FALLEN

What causes all of us to fail to measure up to the image of the glory of God we were created to be, according to Romans 3:23?

- ○ Sin
- ○ Fear
- ○ Death
- ○ Emotion

9 COMPLETE

The process of a believer's transformation into the perfect image of God is gradual. 1 John 3:2 tells us when that process will be completed.

10 WHEN?

When will a Christian finally fully bear God's image?

When they see _____

Which Coat Will You Wear Today? | Colossians 3:9-12

11 | EQUAL IN CHRIST

Like verse 11, Galatians 3:28 also speaks of how all believers are equal in Christ.

12 | WHY?

Why do things like gender, nationality, past religion, and occupation not matter once a person is in Christ?

13 | CHOSEN

Let's look at the three words used to describe Christians in verse 12. First, consider the word translated *elect* or *chosen* (G1588 – eklektos). It means picked out or chosen by God.

14 | SET APART

Next, look at the word translated *holy* (G40 – hagios) which refers to something set apart or consecrated to God, something that is pure.

15 | BELOVED

Finally, look at the word translated *beloved* (G25 – agapaō). It means to love dearly or be fond of.

16 | GOD'S LOVE

When you consider these ways that God thinks about and relates to His people, what is your response?

APPLICATION

1. OFF AND ON

What will it look like in your life today to put off the old, sinful nature and to put on the new, Christ-like nature instead?

2. PREFERENCE

In what ways do you consider certain types of people – rich or poor, male or female, eastern or western – better than others, and how should that change based on God's perspective of people as equal?

CLOSING

We hope this study has given you a clearer understanding of the difference between the old, sinful nature and the new, Christ-like nature, and challenged you to put off the old one and put on the new.

JOURNAL

Write down any additional thoughts that come to mind as a result of this lesson.

Love – The Key to Every Christian VIRTUE

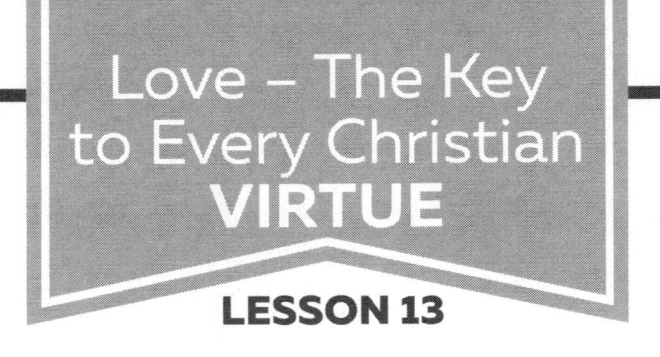

LESSON 13

BIG IDEA

Christians are to put on true love with every other virtue.

PASSAGE

Colossians 3:12-17

TOPIC

Love

INTRODUCTION

Nearly 500 years ago, a soldier was sentenced to death for his crimes. The sentence was to be carried out at the ringing of the evening curfew bell.

Anxiously the prisoner waited for the bell – time crept along more slowly than ever before. He began to think he had lost all sense of time when, to his surprise, the sun began to rise on a new day.

Soon a guard entered the holding cell. The condemned steeled himself for his execution when he heard, "You have been set free."

In answer to his confused face, the guard explained, "Last night the bell that was to sound the hour of your death never rang. The bell man looked to see what was wrong, and found your fiancée clinging to the clapper to keep it from sounding.

"When the general questioned her about it, she showed him her bruised and bleeding hands. Because of her love, you are set free."

It is true love that sacrifices self to do good to another. Colossians 3:12-17 speaks of this kind of love that characterizes a Christian's life and how it will demonstrate itself in so many other virtues.

OBSERVATION

1 PRAY

As you begin to study this passage, pray that God will help you understand it and show you how your life should change because of it.

2 READ FOCUS VERSES

The passage you'll be studying today is Colossians 3:12-17. As you read, notice how many virtues are mentioned.

3 CONTEXT

This passage is part of a longer one that gives more background on how to understand these verses. Read Colossians 3:1-17 and see how today's passage fits into its larger context.

4 | WHO?

What are some of the things that have been said through this larger passage about the people addressed in verses 12-17?

5 | NEW NATURE

What virtues are listed in today's verses that are part of the new nature a Christian is supposed to put on?

Love – The Key to Every Christian Virtue | Colossians 3:12-17

6 KEYWORDS – VIRTUES

Marking each of the virtues that will characterize a Christian who is putting on the new nature will help them stand out each time you read the passage. Use a greater than sign ("**>**") to mark all of the virtues listed in Colossians 3:12-17.

Visit **http://ibible.study/worksheet**
to print out a Bible Worksheet for this study.

7 MATCHING

The way a Christian is to do everything ○ ○ God's Word and His wisdom

Which virtue is most important? ○ ○ Love

Why are Christians supposed to forgive others? ○ ○ Psalms, hymns, and spiritual songs

What is supposed to rule a Christian's heart? ○ ○ In Jesus' Name with thanks to God

What is to live abundantly in a Christian? ○ ○ Because Christ forgave them

Used to teach and admonish each other ○ ○ God's peace

Love – The Key to Every Christian Virtue | Colossians 3:12-17

8 THANKS

Verse 15 commands Christians to give thanks. Verse 17 clarifies how often and to whom. How often are Christians to give thanks, and to whom are they to give it?

Love – The Key to Every Christian Virtue | Colossians 3:12-17

INTERPRETATION

1 — THE NEW NATURE

In the previous study on Colossians 3:9-12, you can study the identity of a Christian's new nature. Today we'll look at its characteristics.

2 — MERCY

James 2:13 gives a poignant reason we should show mercy to others.

3 — KINDNESS

Notice what Ephesians 4:32 says about being kind.

4 — HUMILITY

Philippians 2:5-11 holds up the ultimate example of humility.

Love – The Key to Every Christian Virtue | Colossians 3:12-17

5 WHO?

Who is the ultimate example of humility, according to Scripture?
- ○ Jesus
- ○ Paul
- ○ Moses
- ○ Peter

6 HOW?

How was His humility displayed?

Love – The Key to Every Christian Virtue | Colossians 3:12-17

7 MEEKNESS

Meekness is not a word we use frequently, and so we often misunderstand it. Meekness refers to power under control. This word translated *meek* was used in New Testament times for a Roman war horse that was so well trained it no longer needed blinders as it went into battle. Why were the blinders unnecessary now? Because the horse was so focused on its master and what he wanted that there was no time for it to be spooked by the battle around it.

8 MEEKEST MAN

Numbers 12:3 identifies an outstanding example of meekness.

9 IN YOUR OWN WORDS

Thinking of the examples of Jesus and Moses and the illustration of a well-trained war horse, how would you define meekness in your own words?

10 | REWARD

In Matthew 5:5, Jesus describes the reward for those who live meekly – actively submissive to God's will.

11 | EXAMPLE

Romans 3:21-26 shows us the ultimate example of patience.

12 | FOR UNITY

Ephesians 4:1-3 explains the significance of patience.

13 | PATIENCE

Why is patience so important, and how does God's patience with us put our patience in perspective?

Love – The Key to Every Christian Virtue | Colossians 3:12-17

14 — FORGIVING SPIRIT

Matthew 6:9-15 explains why a believer is forgiving – if a person does not forgive, it shows that they have not been forgiven or do not understand the forgiveness they have been granted. (If you have an extra minute or two, read Jesus' parable about forgiveness in Matthew 18:21-35 also.)

15 — THE BOND OF PERFECTNESS

Colossians 3:14 calls love the bond that ties all the other virtues of the Christian life together. Read the description of love in 1 Corinthians 13:4-7 to find out why.

16 — FIRST AND SECOND

See what Jesus says about love in Matthew 22:37-40.

17 — GOD IS LOVE

1 John 4:8 tells us the most significant thing about love that makes it central to everything else.

18 LOVE

Why is love the most important thing – the thing which ties everything else together?

19 PEACE

Philippians 4:6-7 tells us how a Christian can get the peace which is to rule their hearts.

20 FINDING PEACE

How can a Christian find peace, according to God's Word?

Love – The Key to Every Christian Virtue | Colossians 3:12-17

21 SINGING

Like Colossians 3:16, Ephesians 5:19 speaks of the importance of singing in the Christian life.

22 WHY SING

What are some of the reasons the Bible gives that a Christian should sing?

23 GIVING THANKS

1 Thessalonians 5:18 tells us why Christians should give thanks.

24 BECAUSE...

Why should a Christian be thankful in everything, according to 1 Thessalonians 5:18?

- ○ It's fun
- ○ It's invigorating
- ○ It's good for stirring up a brighter outlook
- ○ It's God's will

25 IN HIS NAME

What does it mean to do everything in the Name of the Lord Jesus?

Love – The Key to Every Christian Virtue | Colossians 3:12-17

26 LIVING FOR JESUS

According to Colossians 3:17, is there any part of an obedient Christian's life which is not lived for God? Why or why not?

APPLICATION

1 | PUT ON LOVE

If you have trusted Christ as your Savior, how are you going to strive to put on love and each of these other virtues today?

2 | IN JESUS' NAME

If you are Christ's, everything you do reflects on Him. It is as if you are saying Jesus Himself would do whatever you are doing because everything you do is in His Name if you are His. How will this reality change the way you live today?

CLOSING

We hope this study has challenged you to put on love with every other virtue of the Christian life.

JOURNAL

Write down any additional thoughts that come to mind as a result of this lesson.

Additional RESOURCES

To aid in your study of this passage, we've placed the following additional resource on our website:

Meekness – This page has a short definition of meekness and some passages that speak of Jesus' meekness.

Visit http://ibible.study/resources

The Christian FAMILY

LESSON 14

BIG IDEA

God has specific instructions for each member of a Christian family so that they can have happy homes and stable lives.

PASSAGE

Colossians 3:18-21

TOPIC

Family

INTRODUCTION

George Whitefield, the famous evangelist, once stayed at the Edwards' home for a few days. After his visit he wrote, "A sweeter couple I have not yet seen." And also added that Sarah Edwards was such a beautiful example of a godly wife it renewed his desire to marry. The next year he was a married man.

Would someone visiting your home desire to have a person like you in their home?

How would you even define a godly husband or wife? What about a godly parent or child? Thankfully, God doesn't leave us to surmise the answers on our own, He provides them directly in His Word. Colossians 3:18-21 gives us a pattern for godly family life which will lead to happy homes and stable lives.

OBSERVATION

1 PRAY

Before studying this passage, ask the Lord to give you understanding and wisdom. His Spirit can open the eyes of your understanding and convict and comfort you through His Word.

2 READ FOCUS VERSES

Today's passage in the book of Colossians is short, but it is powerful. Read Colossians 3:18–21 and notice what kind of relationships it talks about.

3 THEME

What is the theme of this passage? What broad category of relationships are spoken about?

4 | KEYWORD – FAMILY RELATIONSHIPS

Use a heart ("♡") to highlight the words referring to family relationships, like *husband* and *children*, in Colossians 3:18–21.

5 | 4 ROLES

People in four roles within the family are addressed, each in one of the verses of today's passage. What are the four roles addressed?

Wives, husbands, _____, and parents

6 | MATCHING

Relationship of first two people addressed — Love your wife, don't be bitter against her

Relationship of second two people addressed — Don't provoke your children to anger

Command for wives — Obey your parents

Commands for husbands — Parent/child

Command for children — Married

Command for parents — Submit to your own husband in the Lord

The Christian Family | Colossians 3:18-21

7 OBEY

Why are children to obey their parents, according to verse 20?

8 WHY?

Why does God say parents are not to provoke their children to anger?

So they won't become _____

9 CONTEXT

Read Colossians 3:8-17 which appears directly before this passage. Consider how it provides the backdrop for these verses on family relationships.

The Christian Family | Colossians 3:18-21

INTERPRETATION

1 | FAMILY

Why does God deal with the family so specifically in His description of the Christian life?

2 | MORE INFORMATION

Ephesians 5:22–33 gives us more information about the reason for God's instructions to husbands and wives. Read the passage to understand His perspective.

The Christian Family | Colossians 3:18–21

3 | A PICTURE

What relationship is marriage supposed to represent, according to Ephesians 5?

4 | THE WIFE

Since marriage is a picture of the relationship between Jesus Christ and His church, who does the wife represent?

- ○ Jesus Christ
- ○ The church
- ○ The husband
- ○ The wife

The Christian Family | Colossians 3:18-21

5 | THE HUSBAND

Who does the husband have a responsibility to represent in his marriage?
- ○ Jesus Christ
- ○ The church
- ○ The husband
- ○ The wife

6 | THE CURSE

In Genesis 3:16 we see that sinful men and women struggle specifically with God's respective commands for them in marriage – love and submission.

7 | LOVE

How much is a husband supposed to love his wife, according to Ephesians? What is his model?

8 — LOVE LIKE HIS

When we consider the love Jesus Christ had for His bride the church – leaving heaven to live over three decades on earth, being hated and mistreated, finding His friends false to Him, going hungry and unsheltered, being unjustly tried, facing death without cause, having nails driven through His hands and feet and a crown of thorns into His head, giving up His life and dying for her – how can a man demonstrate this kind of love for his wife? Could there be any personal sacrifice or any discomfort too great to bear for her?

9 — SUBMISSION

Why do you think God so specifically clarifies that a wife is to submit to her *own* husband?

The Christian Family | Colossians 3:18-21

10 — AS IS FITTING

Why does God say wives should submit to their husbands as it would please the Lord? How does this phrase clarify the attitude and extent of the submission God is commanding?

11 — AGREEMENT

Biblically, can a husband and wife agree that he doesn't have to sacrificially love her and she doesn't have to submit in some areas? Why or why not?

12 FURTHER EXPLAINED

The verses about parents and children are further explained in Ephesians 6:1-4.

13 DISOBEDIENCE

According to these verses in Colossians and Ephesians, when may a child disobey their parents (assuming that their parents are not telling them to sin against God)?

○ Never
○ Sometimes
○ When they feel like it
○ If someone else's parent thinks it's a good idea

14 A PERFECT SON

We see a perfect example of obedience in the Lord Jesus as a boy in Luke 2:51-52.

15 | THE SON OF GOD

The ultimate example of obedience is found in Jesus' relationship to His heavenly Father. We see this throughout Scripture, but it is vividly portrayed in Philippians 2:5-12.

16 | DISCOURAGED

Take a moment to look at the word translated *discouraged* (G120 – athymeō) which God uses to describe what happens when a parent provokes their child to anger. It means to be broken in spirit, disheartened, discouraged.

17 | A PARENT'S RESPONSIBILITY

Notice how accountable God holds parents for the actions of the children in their home in 1 Timothy 3:4-5.

18 — ULTIMATE FATHER

Who is the ultimate example of fatherhood in the Bible?

- ○ Adam
- ○ David
- ○ God
- ○ Peter

The Christian Family | Colossians 3:18-21

APPLICATION

1 CHRIST AND THE CHURCH

How does seeing marriage as a picture of the relationship between Jesus Christ and the church change your perspective on marriage?

2 ROLE MODELS

As you saw in today's study, family relationships reflect relationships with God. When you want to dig deeper into how to relate to your family as a Christian, the biblical models provide answers. If you are a wife, you can study how the church is to relate to Jesus Christ. If you are a husband, you can study how Christ relates to the church.

If you are a child, you can see how Jesus Christ relates to His Father. If you are a father, you can study how God parents His children. What family relationships do you have, and how do you need to change the way you are relating to your family to properly reflect God's pattern?

The Christian Family | Colossians 3:18-21

CLOSING

We hope this study has helped you better understand God's pattern and purpose for each member of the family.

JOURNAL

Write down any additional thoughts that come to mind as a result of this lesson.

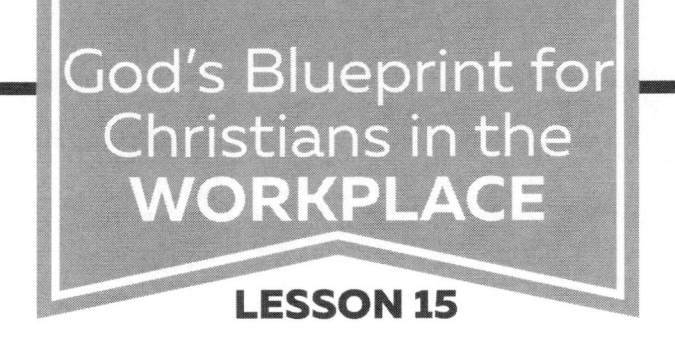

God's Blueprint for Christians in the WORKPLACE

LESSON 15

BIG IDEA

A Christian is to work for Christ at their place of business whether they are an employer or an employee.

PASSAGE

Colossians 3:22–4:1

TOPIC

Work

INTRODUCTION

In the Welsh countryside was a church that had been growing steadily for several years. The pastor, of course, was very pleased with the growth, but he had a suspicion they would see more growth if more of his people faithfully shared the hope of the gospel with those they knew and met.

One Sunday evening he decided to test his theory. He asked everyone to stand who had been won to Christ by someone else in the room. There were scores of them. Those who had been members for decades gasped as they saw growth they'd vaguely sensed but until now had not seen. One by one, the pastor asked those standing to name the person who had led them to Jesus.

Most named one man – an uneducated coal miner who had shoulders wider than the chapel door frame and hands that could double as dinner plates.

The pastor asked several people that this man had reached how he did it. Each replied with a similar story.

The miner had set out to be a witness for Jesus Christ after his conversion. He knew there wasn't much he could do, but he could be the best worker in the place. Some of the others complained, once a boss even reprimanded him, but the miner always replied that he was working for Jesus now and he couldn't slow down.

Eventually, his coworkers stopped cursing at him when he mentioned the Lord. After several years, he had won their respect by continuing to work for Jesus. They began to ask the miner about his faith. One at a time he told them of the precious blood of Jesus which cleanses from every sin. He shared the overwhelming love of God that makes sinners His children.

And so it was that so many of them were now faithful members of the church – won in part by the way a simple man worked.

Colossians 3:22-4:1 gives us a blueprint for working as Christians. Whether we are an employee or an employer, God has guidelines and principles to show His people how to be a testimony in the way they work. Are you ready to work so that people can see that you are working for a new Master?

OBSERVATION

1 — PRAY

Before reading and studying this passage, ask the Lord to give you wisdom and understanding through it. Pray that He will show you errors in your thinking and what you've been taught. Ask Him to show you specific ways you can live these truths in your own daily life.

2 — READ FOCUS VERSES

Read Colossians 3:22-4:1 and notice to whom these verses are especially addressed.

God's Blueprint for Christians in the Workplace | Colossians 3:22-4:1

3 — TO WHOM?

Who is the main audience of these verses?

4 — KEYWORD – EMPLOYER OR EMPLOYEE

Use a dollar sign ("$") to mark the words referring to employers and employees in Colossians 3:22–4:1.

Visit **http://ibible.study/worksheet** to print out a Bible Worksheet for this study.

5 — CONTEXT

Colossians 3:1–4, which opens this discussion of what it looks like to live as a Christian in every area of life, tells us more about the employers and employees addressed in today's passage.

God's Blueprint for Christians in the Workplace | Colossians 3:22–4:1

6 DIFFERENT

What should set these employers and employees apart from the regular worker, according to Colossians 3:1-4?

- ○ Their pride in their work
- ○ Their sense of honor
- ○ Their status as risen with Christ
- ○ Their natural diligence

7 INSTRUCTIONS

What are the two instructions God gives to employees in verses 22-23?

_____ your masters and do everything _____ to the Lord.

God's Blueprint for Christians in the Workplace | Colossians 3:22-4:1

8 EXPLAINED

How does God explain what it means to obey your boss in the second half of verse 22?

9 ULTIMATE BOSS

Who does a Christian employee ultimately seek to please when they work, according to verse 23?

- ○ Self
- ○ Boss
- ○ Pastor
- ○ God

God's Blueprint for Christians in the Workplace | Colossians 3:22-4:1

10 — A GOOD REASON

What reason does God give for these commands in verse 24?

11 — WHY?

What other reason does God give for these commands in verse 25?

12 — EMPLOYERS

What command does God give to employers in Colossians 4:1?

Give your employees what is _____ and _____.

God's Blueprint for Christians in the Workplace | Colossians 3:22–4:1

13 WHY?

Why are employers given this command, according to this verse?

14 WHO?

Who does this passage say a Christian employer is ultimately supposed to please?

- ○ Self
- ○ Boss
- ○ Pastor
- ○ God

God's Blueprint for Christians in the Workplace | Colossians 3:22–4:1

INTERPRETATION

1 — EYESERVICE

In your own words, what does it mean to work in singleness of heart to the Lord and not only when people can see you?

2 — EVERYTHING

Employees are told to obey in everything – and not just when the boss is looking. But is there an exception to this? Notice what Peter says with God's approval in Acts 4:19.

3 — GOD RATHER THAN MEN

Read Acts 5:29 and notice how similar it is to our passage in Colossians.

God's Blueprint for Christians in the Workplace | Colossians 3:22–4:1

4 BIBLICALLY SPEAKING

The Bible commands people to obey government and employers. According to Acts 5:29, is there ever a time when God wants us to disobey someone whose authority He has told us to obey? If so, when?

5 WHY?

If we think about the Bible's reasons why a Christian is supposed to obey authority this exception makes sense. Why should a Christian obey God instead of someone God typically wants them to obey when that authority disagrees with God?

God's Blueprint for Christians in the Workplace | Colossians 3:22-4:1

6 — DILIGENTLY

Verse 23 urges us to work diligently. Notice what Ecclesiastes 9:10 says about this.

7 — INHERITANCE

In verse 24, Christian employees are promised an inheritance from the Lord if they work for Jesus Christ's sake whether or not their boss is a Christian. Read about that inheritance in 1 Corinthians 3:11-15.

8 — REWARD

Just like there is reward for doing good, there is reward for doing evil in verse 25. What does it mean that God does not prefer one person over another when He rewards for doing wrong?

God's Blueprint for Christians in the Workplace | Colossians 3:22-4:1

9 | THINKING RIGHTLY

1 Timothy 6:1-2 teaches employees how to think about their bosses.

10 | THE GOOD AND THE BAD

1 Peter 2:18 also speaks of the relationship between an employee and their employer.

11 | IN YOUR OWN WORDS

How would you restate what these passage say in your own words?

12 | SIMILARITIES

Take a look at Ephesians 6:5-9. Notice the similarities between the passages.

God's Blueprint for Christians in the Workplace | Colossians 3:22-4:1

13 COMMAND

What command is given to employers in Ephesians 6 that is not specifically noted in Colossians?

- ○ Don't threaten them
- ○ Pay them
- ○ Speak kindly
- ○ Ask about their family

14 ULTIMATE AUTHORITY

Ephesians further underlines the importance of understanding who is the ultimate authority. How will understanding that God is the ultimate authority affect the employer and employee respectively?

God's Blueprint for Christians in the Workplace | Colossians 3:22-4:1

APPLICATION

1 FOR THE LORD

Whether you are an employee or an employer, what needs to change about the way you work so that you work consistently for the Lord and not just when others can see you?

2 WILLING?

Are you willing to lose your job to maintain your integrity and obey God rather than men? How can you commit that to God today?

God's Blueprint for Christians in the Workplace | Colossians 3:22-4:1

3 WORSHIP

If you are a Christian, how will you do your work as worship today?

God's Blueprint for Christians in the Workplace | Colossians 3:22–4:1

CLOSING

We hope this study has helped you understand God's blueprint for the Christian in the workplace and encouraged you to work for the Lord.

JOURNAL

Write down any additional thoughts that come to mind as a result of this lesson.

Additional RESOURCES

To aid in your study of this passage, we've placed the following additional resources on our website:

An Example – This short clip shows one way a person might recognize God as the ultimate authority while still respecting earthly authorities as much as possible.

Work as Worship – Here's a short video that explains how your job in the workplace is worship if you do it according to the principles and commands of these verses.

Visit http://ibible.study/resources

4 Directions for a Healthy Christian LIFE

LESSON 16

BIG IDEA

A healthy Christian life is one of prayer and thanksgiving, wisdom, redeeming the time, and speaking with grace.

PASSAGE

Colossians 4:2-6

TOPIC

Christian Life

INTRODUCTION

A young man was called to pastor a large church in Philadelphia. After his first sermon, a man from the congregation approached him. "You're pretty young to be pastor of this church," he said, "but you preach the gospel, and I'm going to help you all I can. I'm going to pray for you that you may have the Holy Spirit's power upon you. Two others have covenanted to join with me in prayer for you."

Every Sunday before the service these three men gathered to pray. Soon their number swelled to five, then ten, fifty, until hundreds of Christians gathered each Sunday morning to ask for God's power on their preacher and in the service.

You will not be surprised that God added many souls to that church. Nor will it be a surprise that the pastor, Wilbur Chapman, became a mighty preacher and evangelist.

In Colossians 4:2-6 Paul asks the Colossian Christians to pray for him in a similar way. Study this passage to learn how to live a healthy Christian life of effective prayer, wisdom, and grace.

OBSERVATION

1 PRAY

Before studying this passage of Scripture, ask the God who wrote it to make it plain to you and to show you how He wants to change your life through it.

2 READ FOCUS VERSES

As you read Colossians 4:2-6, pay attention to the structure of the passage.

3 4 COMMANDS

1. Continue and watch in _____

2. _____ in wisdom with those of the world.

3. _____ the time.

4. Speak with _____

4 Directions for a Healthy Christian Life | Colossians 4:2-6

4   KEYWORDS – VERBS

Marking the main action words in this passage will make the structure of the passage clear and easy to study. Use a double arrow ("⟹") to mark the five main action words in Colossians 4:2-6. There are two for the first command, and one for each of the others.

Visit **http://ibible.study/worksheet**
to print out a Bible Worksheet for this study.

5   GIVING THANKS

What is a significant part of biblical prayer, according to verse 2?

- ○ Petitions
- ○ Weeping
- ○ Thanksgiving
- ○ Hope

6 MATCHING

Prayer is requested for (v. 3) ○   ○ Imprisoned

What to pray for ministers of the gospel (vv. 3-4) ○   ○ Clearly as God directs

Paul's condition because he preached the gospel (v. 3) ○   ○ Opportunity, boldness, and clarity

How the gospel should be presented (v. 4) ○   ○ Paul and Timothy

7 WALK IN WISDOM

A Christian needs special wisdom to know how to interact with whom in verse 5?
- ○ Other Christians
- ○ Unbelievers
- ○ No one
- ○ Everyone

8 ANALOGY

What physical analogy is used to describe godly speech in verse 6?

Seasoned with _____

9 HOW OFTEN?

How often is a Christian's speech to be gracious?
- ○ Sometimes
- ○ Always
- ○ Never

10 WHY?

According to verse 6, why is it important for Christians to speak with grace?

4 Directions for a Healthy Christian Life | Colossians 4:2-6

INTERPRETATION

1 | CONTINUE

Verse 2 commands that Christians continue in prayer. Take a look at the word translated *continue* or *devoted* (G4342 – proskartereō) to get a fuller sense of the way a Christian is to pray. It means to be constantly diligent, to persevere, to attend to continually, to give unremitting care to, to be courageous for and steadfast in without fainting.

2 | PRAY AND GIVE THANKS

Notice that 1 Thessalonians 5:17-18 also pairs praying and giving thanks.

3 | THANKS IN PRAYER

Philippians 4:6-7 gives the same emphasis to thanksgiving in prayer.

4 | WHY?

Why is giving thanks such a significant part of biblical prayer?

5 | THE LABOR OF PRAYER

If we go down a few verses to Colossians 4:12 we see an interesting description of Epaphras' prayer life.

6 | IN YOUR OWN WORDS

In your own words, what does Colossians 4:12 teach you about prayer and how seriously you should take it?

7) WORDS OF BOLDNESS

If anyone was an effective, bold evangelist with the blessing of God on his ministry, it was the apostle Paul. But in Colossians 4 he asks believers to pray that the Lord will open doors for him to share the gospel and give him the words to say when those opportunities come. Notice how similar his request to the Ephesian church is in Ephesians 6:18-20.

8) SPECIFICS

In 2 Thessalonians 3:1-2, we are given some very specific ways to pray for those who minister and preach the word.

9) PRAYING MIGHTILY

What are some of the specific things you should pray for the ministers of the gospel you know?

10 CLARITY

In Colossians 4:4, Paul asks the believers to pray that he will be able to share the gospel with clarity. Notice what 1 Peter 3:15 says about this.

11 WHO?

Are people like Paul and other pastors and evangelists the only ones who need prayer for open doors and clarity so they can share the gospel? If not, who else does?

12 WISDOM AND TIME MANAGEMENT

The first part of Ephesians 5 instructs Christians as they interact with unbelievers. Notice how similar Ephesians 5:15-17 is to Colossians 4:5.

4 Directions for a Healthy Christian Life | Colossians 4:2-6

13 RELATION

Why are the two ideas of interacting properly to the world and redeeming time so closely related in these passages?

14 CHRISTIAN SPEECH

The descriptions "with grace" and "seasoned with salt" provide a framework for understanding how God wants His people to speak. "Always" tells us that there is never a time a Christian may speak without grace (Ephesians 4:29). "With grace" points us to the perfect example of Christian speech by reminding us that Jesus' speech was gracious (Luke 4:22). "Seasoned with salt" indicates that our speech is to be pleasant, purifying, effective, healing, and interesting – just like salt which adds flavor, makes food pleasant, cleanses and heals wounds, and is effective for many other things including preserving foods.

15 — A READY ANSWER

We already looked at 1 Peter 3:15 which talks about having a ready answer just as Colossians 4:6 does. What does this mean?

16 — CHRISTIAN COMMUNICATION

Notice what Ephesians 4:29 says about a Christian's communication.

17 — WHEN?

When we compare the way Ephesians 4:29 commands "never" and Colossians 4:6 "always," is there ever a time when a Christian has a good enough excuse to speak corruptly or not be gracious? Why or why not?

APPLICATION

1. PRAYING

How should your prayer life change based on what you've seen from Scripture?

2. REDEEMING THE TIME

What are some ways the Lord wants you to redeem your time today?

4 Directions for a Healthy Christian Life | Colossians 4:2-6

3 COMMUNICATION

How will you begin to hold the things you say accountable to this passage of Scripture?

4 Directions for a Healthy Christian Life | Colossians 4:2-6

CLOSING

We hope this study has encouraged and equipped you to live a healthy Christian life full of prayer and thanksgiving, wisdom, redeeming the time, and speaking with grace.

JOURNAL

Write down any additional thoughts that come to mind as a result of this lesson.

Additional RESOURCES

To aid in your study of this passage, we've placed the following additional resource on our website:

Christian Speech – This short exposition of Colossians 4:6 is very helpful.

Visit http://ibible.study/resources

Paul's HELPERS

LESSON 17

BIG IDEA

Paul gives us a glimpse into the lives of some of his faithful helpers – a glimpse which will encourage and challenge Christians to work with others in the gospel.

PASSAGE

Colossians 4:7-11

TOPIC

Christian Life

INTRODUCTION

Once a famous entertainer was asked to appear with a show for the troops. He agreed on the condition that he be allowed to leave for another appointment after a single monologue.

He stepped on stage to deliver the monologue, then performed another act, and another. The applause grew steadily.

Finally, after half an hour, the entertainer came backstage.

Someone asked him, "Didn't you have to leave after a few minutes?"

"Yes, I did have to go. You can see on the front row the reason I remained."

There sitting together were two men – one had lost his right arm and the other his left arm so they were clapping together.

This kind of teamwork is not just critical to enjoying life, but to maintaining it. For example, on hot days a bee hive will divide its occupants in half. One half will remain at the hive beating their wings to keep the hive cool. The other half will go out and gather pollen for honey. The next day the teams will switch – working together to keep the colony alive.

In Colossians 4:7-11, we see some men who worked as a team to do God's work. Study the passage to be challenged in the way you work with others.

OBSERVATION

1 PRAY

Before studying this passage, humble yourself before the Lord and ask Him to open your eyes to understand His truth.

2 READ FOCUS VERSES

Read Colossians 4:7-11 and notice the people Paul talks about and what he emphasizes about each of them.

3 KEYWORD – NAMES

Underline ("_") the name of each person Paul mentions in Colossians 4:7-11.

Visit **http://ibible.study/worksheet** to print out a Bible Worksheet for this study.

4 | HOW MANY?

How many people are named in this passage?

- ○ 6
- ○ 7
- ○ 8
- ○ 9

5 | A REPORT

What is Tychicus going to tell the church in Colossae?

- ○ How he is doing
- ○ How Paul is doing
- ○ How the church in Rome is doing
- ○ How the church in general is doing

6 TYCHICUS

How does Paul describe Tychicus?

Beloved _____

_____ minister

_____

7 WHY?

Why did Paul send Tychicus to Colossae?

8 ONESIMUS

How does Paul introduce Onesimus?

Faithful and _____ brother who is from among you

9 | ROLE

What is Onesimus' role, according to verse 9?

- ○ To be refreshed by the church
- ○ To strengthen his faith
- ○ To relieve Paul
- ○ To help help Tychicus give the Colossians an update

10 | WHO'S NEXT?

Who is mentioned next in the passage?

_____

11 | ARISTARCHUS

How is Aristarchus spoken of?

Paul's fellow _____

Paul's Helpers | Colossians 4:7-11

12 MATCHING

Sent greetings through this letter ○   ○ Uncle and nephew

Barnabas and Mark were ○   ○ Jews

Aristarchus, Mark, and Justus were all ○   ○ Aristarchus and Mark

13 DESCRIPTION

In verse 11, how does Paul describe all of the people named in this passage?

Paul's Helpers | Colossians 4:7-11

INTERPRETATION

1 — HOW WE ARE

Notice that Paul also sends Tychicus to tell the Ephesian church how things are going with him in Ephesians 6:21-22.

2 — THE REASON

Why does Paul say he was sending someone to let the Christians in these churches know how he was doing?

3 | COMFORT

What kind of man must Tychicus have been for Paul to know he would comfort these believers' hearts?

4 | ONESIMUS

Paul also sends Onesimus to bring this report of how things are going. Philemon 1:10-17 gives us an interesting background on his story.

5 | IN YOUR OWN WORDS

In your own words, what is Onesimus' story?

Paul's Helpers | Colossians 4:7-11

6 ARISTARCHUS

Read what Acts 19:29 says about Aristarchus.

7 COMPANION

What do we learn about Aristarchus from Acts 19:29?

8 MARK

Acts 15:37-40 tells us about an interesting period in Paul and Mark's relationship.

9 | A CHANGE

By the time Paul was writing 2 Timothy 4:11, the relationship was much improved.

10 | SIGNIFICANT

In light of these passages, why is the way Paul speaks of Mark here in Colossians so significant?

11 | BARNABAS

Barnabas was one of the first Christians to welcome Paul into the church after his conversion. Read about it in Acts 9:26-27.

Paul's Helpers | Colossians 4:7-11

12 CIRCUMCISION

Circumcision was a symbol of the covenant God made with Abraham and his descendants. It set Jews apart from Gentiles and the term was often used to signify a Jewish person as in Ephesians 2:11-13.

13 FELLOW WORKERS

Stop to think about what Paul calls these people – his *fellow workers* (G4904 – synergos). This word means a companion in labor, a coworker.

14 WORKING TOGETHER

Using the analogy of gardening or farming, Paul speaks of the way Christ's servants work together in His kingdom in 1 Corinthians 3:6-9.

15 — THE ONE

Who does 1 Corinthians 3:6-9 teach us Christians ultimately work with?

- ◯ God
- ◯ Each other
- ◯ Pastors
- ◯ Missionaries

16 — MEANING

What are Christians working together to do, according to Colossians 4:11 and 1 Corinthians 3:6-9?

Paul's Helpers | Colossians 4:7-11

17 COMFORT

Read 1 Thessalonians 3:7-8 to discover what was the greatest comfort to Paul.

18 COMFORTERS

What does it mean that these people Paul mentions in Colossians 4 comforted him?

Paul's Helpers | Colossians 4:7-11

APPLICATION

1. WORKING TOGETHER

If you are a Christian, how can you work together with other Christians to build the kingdom of God today?

2. COMFORTER

How can you be a comfort to other Christians this week?

Paul's Helpers | Colossians 4:7-11

CLOSING

We hope this study has challenged you to work together with other Christians to do God's work.

JOURNAL

Write down any additional thoughts that come to mind as a result of this lesson.

Examples of Faithful SERVANTS

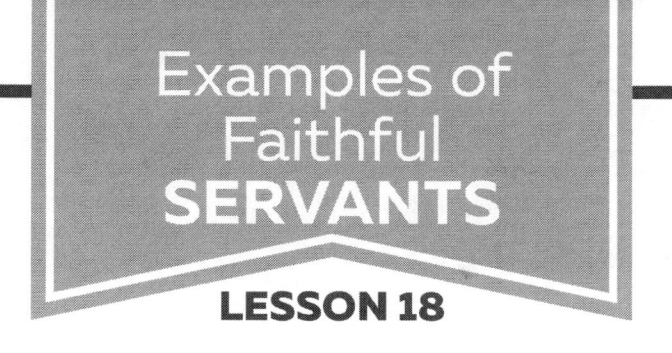

LESSON 18

BIG IDEA

Christians, regardless of their role, serve the Lord and His people faithfully.

PASSAGE

Colossians 4:12-18

TOPIC

Christian Life

INTRODUCTION

As the Second World War raged in Europe, England needed more coal. Winston Churchill called a meeting with the labor leaders and vividly described a day at the end of the war when the men who had won the war would parade through Piccadilly Circus.

First, he said, would come sailors who had kept the seas open to the ships. Next would come soldiers who had fought with valor. After them would be the pilots who had defeated the Luftwaffe. Behind these heroes that everyone recognized would follow men covered in soot and sweat. The crowd would ask, "Where were these men in those critical days of fighting?"

Each of the miners with heads held high would stand and reply together, "We were deep in the earth with our faces to the coal."

In Colossians 4:12–18, we get a glimpse of several men who served God's people in various roles. Some were more visible than others, but each had a critical role to play in building Christ's church. Study this passage to learn more about these examples of faithful service and be challenged to serve.

OBSERVATION

1 PRAY

Seek the Lord in prayer and ask Him to give you wisdom and an understanding heart as you study today's passage.

2 READ FOCUS VERSES

Today we look at the last seven verses of Colossians. Read Colossians 4:12-18 and pay attention to how the book closes.

3 CONTEXT

Start in Colossians 4:7 and read through verse 18 to get a better feel for these two closely related passages.

4 | KEYWORDS – PEOPLE

God, through Paul, highlights many people in this passage. Underline ("_") the names of each of the people and churches mentioned in this passage to help them stand out to you (don't forget the pronouns, like *them* and *those*, which indicate a church of Christians). Think how significant God's people are to Him since He singles out so many of them in the Bible for us to read about generations later.

Visit **http://ibible.study/worksheet**
to print out a Bible Worksheet for this study.

5 | HOW MANY?

How many people and groups are named in today's passage?

- ○ 8
- ○ 9
- ○ 10
- ○ 11

Examples of Faithful Servants | Colossians 4:12–18

6 CITIES

Which cities are mentioned in this passage because they have believers and churches in them?

Colossae, Laodicea, and _____

7 OCCUPATION

Whose occupation is mentioned and what was it?

8 MATCHING

Hosted a church meeting in his house ○   ○ Colossians

Was urged to fulfill the ministry he had received ○   ○ Epaphras

Were to remember Paul's bonds ○   ○ Archippus

Was diligently praying for the believers in Colossae ○   ○ Nymphas

Examples of Faithful Servants | Colossians 4:12-18

INTERPRETATION

1 — EVERY ONE

What does God teach us by mentioning so many people in this passage of Scripture?

2 — EPAPHRAS

Colossians 1:3-8 also speaks of Epaphras.

3 — MENTIONED

Epaphras is mentioned again in Philemon 1:23-24.

Examples of Faithful Servants | Colossians 4:12-18

4 SUMMARIZE

In your own words, how would you describe Epaphras based on these passages?

5 FERVENT

James 5:16-18 speaks of fervent prayer.

6 WHAT?

God includes Epaphras' prayer for these believers he loved as a model for us when we pray for other believers. What does Colossians 4:12 tell us Epaphras was praying for these Christians?

That they would _____ perfect and _____ in the will of God

7 ZEAL

What did it look like for Epaphras to be zealous for the Christians in these three cities?

8 LUKE

Luke, mentioned in verse 14, wrote two books of the Bible – Luke and Acts – and frequently travelled with Paul. What are some reasons it might have been significant to Paul that Luke was a doctor?

9 DEMAS

Read what is said about Demas at a later time in 2 Timothy 4:10.

Examples of Faithful Servants | Colossians 4:12-18

10 SIMILAR STORY

Jesus explains why people will fall away using a parable in Luke 8:4-15.

11 CHANGE

What happened to this once seemingly genuine believer, according to Scripture?

12 LAODICEA

God did not preserve Paul's letter to the Laodiceans, so we know that it was not inspired because God promises to preserve His Word. However, there is an inspired message to the church of Laodicea in Revelation 3:14-22. As you read those verse, think about the similarities between them and the book of Colossians.

13 — MINISTRY

1 Timothy 4:6 defines a good minister.

14 — GOOD MINISTER

What defines a good minister, according to Scripture?

15 — FULFILLED

Paul was an example of a man who fulfilled the ministry that was given to him by God. See what he says about this as he challenges another young minister – Timothy – in 2 Timothy 4:5-8.

16 FINISHED

What does it mean to fulfill the ministry God has given a person?

17 SUFFERING

Similar to Colossians 4:18, Hebrews 13:3 issues a command to remember the suffering of Christians who are being persecuted for their faith.

18 WHY?

Why is it important that we remember those who are suffering for their faith?

Examples of Faithful Servants | Colossians 4:12-18

19 — GRACE

Paul ends many of his Epistles with a similar benediction and prayer that God's grace would be with them. What does it mean?

Examples of Faithful Servants | Colossians 4:12-18

APPLICATION

1 | FERVENT PRAYER

For whom will you pray like Epaphras did for the Colossians – fervently interceding for their spiritual health and growth?

2 | LOVING THE WORLD

You might look like a Christian on the outside, but are you like Demas on the inside? Does something on this earth mean more to you than everything else? Do you love the Savior more than the comforts of this life? How do you know?

Examples of Faithful Servants | Colossians 4:12-18

3 | MINISTRY

How are you going to fulfill the ministry that God has given you today?

Examples of Faithful Servants | Colossians 4:12-18

CLOSING

We hope you have been challenged and inspired by these examples of faithful service to do faithfully whatever God has called you to do.

JOURNAL

Write down any additional thoughts that come to mind as a result of this lesson.

Additional RESOURCES

To aid in your study of this passage, we've placed the following additional resources on our website:

3 Cities – You can see the three cities mentioned in verse 13 on this map.
Luke – You can learn more about Luke here.

Visit http://ibible.study/resources

APPENDIX

INDUCTIVE BIBLE STUDY BOOK OUTLINE

BOOK NAME

Chapter/Verse(s)	Summary
(i.e. Gen 1:1-2)	(i.e. "God creates heaven and earth")

Download a free PDF of this form at **http://ibible.study/dsgresources**

INDUCTIVE BIBLE STUDY BOOK OUTLINE

BOOK NAME	
Chapter/Verse(s)	**Summary**
(i.e. Gen 1:1-2)	*(i.e. "God creates heaven and earth")*

Download a free PDF of this form at ***http://ibible.study/dsgresources***

SUGGESTED MARKINGS

Keyword	Marking
Beware	Triangle with exclamation mark in center ("⚠")
Employer or Employee	Dollar sign ("$")
Family Relationships	Heart ("♡")
Hope	Plus sign ("+")
Jesus Christ	Cross ("†")
Kill and Take Off	Up arrow with double strikethrough ("⇑")
Mystery	Question mark ("?")
Names/People	Underline ("_")
Paul	Large p ("P")
Pray	Star ("★")
Put Off and Put On	Clockwise arrow ("↻")
Reconcile	Up arrow–down arrow ("↑↓")
Risen	Up arrow ("↑")
Sin and Flesh	Large x ("X")
Verbs	Double arrow ("⟹")
Virtues	Greater than sign (">")

Appendix

STUDIES BY TOPIC

Topic	Title	Page
Christian Life	4 Directions for a Healthy Christian Life	284
Christian Life	Examples of Faithful Servants	317
Christian Life	Paul's Helpers	300
Christian Life	The Minister's Role	116
Christian Life	What Does It Look Like to Be Risen with Christ?	187
Christian Life	Which Coat Will You Wear Today?	219
Family	The Christian Family	250
Freedom	The True Freedom of a Christian	171
Gospel	The Mystery of the Gospel	97
Hope	Hope Changes Everything	21
Jesus Christ	The One with First Place	58
Jesus Christ	Who Jesus Christ Is to a Believer	137
Love	Love – The Key to Every Christian Virtue	232
Prayer	A Glimpse into an Effective Prayer Life	41
Salvation	Reconciled by the Cross of Christ	79
Sin	How a Christian Treats Sin	202
Victory	The 4 Ways Christians Have Victory over Sin	156
Work	God's Blueprint for Christians in the Workplace	266

STUDIES BY PASSAGE

Colossians	Title	Page
1:1-8	Hope Changes Everything	21
1:9-12	A Glimpse into an Effective Prayer Life	41
1:13-18	The One with First Place	58
1:19-23	Reconciled by the Cross of Christ	79
1:24-29	The Mystery of the Gospel	97
2:1-5	The Minister's Role	116
2:6-10	Who Jesus Christ Is to a Believer	137
2:11-15	The 4 Ways Christians Have Victory over Sin	156
2:16-23	The True Freedom of a Christian	171
3:1-4	What Does It Look Like to Be Risen with Christ?	187
3:5-8	How a Christian Treats Sin	202
3:9-12	Which Coat Will You Wear Today?	219
3:12-17	Love – The Key to Every Christian Virtue	232
3:18-21	The Christian Family	250
3:22-4:1	God's Blueprint for Christians in the Workplace	266
4:2-6	4 Directions for a Healthy Christian Life	284
4:7-11	Paul's Helpers	300
4:12-18	Examples of Faithful Servants	317

Appendix

Additional RESOURCES

At Inductive Bible Study LLC, our mission is simple – "make disciples of all nations" (Matt. 28:19). We are committed to providing high quality tools, resources, and training to assist Christ's church in fulfilling the Great Commission.

Also available:

Stop Reading, Start Studying
Inductive Bible Study Method Explained
Do you want to know God more intimately? Do you desire to "get in the Word" but don't know how? Has your Bible been collecting dust more than impacting your life? Are you tired of relying on others to tell you what God says and want to study the Bible yourself? This is the book for you!

Book
The premier book on how to enrich your study of God's Word using the Inductive Bible Study method!
ISBN: 978-0-9970743-0-7

Student Workbook
This five-lesson study provides practical steps on how to study the Bible inductively, memorize & meditate on Scripture, and pray effectively.
ISBN: 978-0-9970743-5-2

Leader Guide
This guide empowers small group leaders with discussion starters, background commentary and easy to follow lesson plans.
ISBN: 978-0-9970743-4-5

Children's Edition: Searching for God's Hidden Treasure
It's never too early to begin teaching children to study God's Word! This workbook provides five easy to follow lessons that teach children how to explore the hidden treasures of the Bible.
ISBN: 978-0-9970743-8-3

About the AUTHORS

HENRY JACKSON III

Henry Jackson III, a bondservant of Jesus Christ. He is a native of Memphis, TN, who now calls Atlanta, GA his home. Henry primarily utilizes his spiritual gifts of teaching and leadership at Elizabeth Baptist Church in Atlanta, GA, where he currently serves as the Children & Youth Spiritual Formation Director. Henry enjoys spending time with his darling wife Vanessa and son Henry IV, kayaking, mountain-bike riding, and playing racquetball.

Henry is the founder of Inductive Bible Study LLC, an organization that empowers individuals to grow in their faith by enabling them to study the Bible inductively using their favorite mobile device. Find out more at InductiveBibleStudyApp.com.

As a Myasthenia Gravis (MG) survivor, Henry is a living testimony of God's healing power. Each day that God gives him the strength, he is constantly pursuing ways to glorify God and to make Him known to the world. A portion of the proceeds from the sales of his books are donated to the Myasthenia Gravis Foundation of America, Inc. Find out more at Myasthenia.org.

CHRISTINA JOY HOMMES

Christina Joy Hommes is a joyful servant of Jesus Christ who loves to learn and help others discover how God guides our daily lives through His Word. She writes and creates tools to encourage Christians and help them live and share their faith every day.

Christina is the author of several Bible studies and discipleship resources. Her goal in each is to encourage readers to love God more and to help bring the Bible to life so they can understand, apply, and share it with confidence. She loves working with ministries and churches to help them reach people with the hope of the gospel. Find out more at HopeRefined.com.

Since earning her M.A. in Biblical Studies, Christina has led women's Bible studies and teaches online. She lives near Nashville, TN and enjoys reading, traveling, playing the piano, and spending time with her family.

Made in the USA
Columbia, SC
09 August 2022